TO LOVE THE SLUMDOG

My Journey Serving the "Untouchables" – The Dalit

Nanci Ricks

INTERMEDIA PUBLISHING GROUP

WWW.INTERMEDIAPUB.COM

to Love the Slumdog

Copyright © 2009 Nanci Ricks
Printed in the United States

Published by:
Intermedia Publishing Group
PO Box 2825
Peoria, AZ 85380

www.intermediapub.com

ISBN 978-1-935529-18-7

DEDICATION

This little girl is often called a "slumdog"—she lives in a slum in India and she comes from the caste of people who are thought to be the "dogs" of Indian society. The people in this caste of course would rather be known by more uplifting, less disrespectful names. They are working hard to overcome such disparagement, even by publicly criticizing the popular movie "Slumdog Millionaire" for its title. You may never have heard of slumdogs before the movie, but you probably have known them as the Untouchables, another dishonorable title. The very word warns you to avoid this group of people: don't touch them, don't go near them, don't interact with them. They are

Dirty, Different, Denigrated.

I know these people as the Dalit, an ancient Indian Marathi word meaning "ground" or "broken into pieces." They have adopted this word to describe themselves because it is a depiction of their situation and not a value judgment of who they are as people. They want to communicate that they have more worth than their society gives them.

I'm sure this little girl has been called a slumdog often enough. She is a beggar needing to make money from tourists while her pimp waits around the corner to make sure she gives him everything she has collected. But her main interest is not in being called a slumdog, or her occupation as a "beggar," or even her responsibility to the pimp—her main interest is that she is noticed and valued, for the nice stranger on the street to admire the new henna on her hand: "Isn't it beautiful?"

THIS BOOK IS DEDICATED TO ALL THE PRECIOUS LITTLE CHILDREN WHO WANT TO BE VALUED AS SOMETHING BEAUTIFUL WHILE THEY LIVE ON THE STREETS AND HEAR UGLY NAMES SHOUTED AT THEM.

I would also like to dedicate this book to four distinct groups of people—

The Dalits, who live in a social situation that condemns them to the largest form of slavery in the world today. It has been my privilege to enter your world and tell your story to anyone who will listen.

To the activists worldwide who have heard the Dalits' cry—who are not simply a voice for the voiceless, but who connect the cry to their own voice, empowering the Dalits to express themselves in ways that will lead to their emancipation.

To my friends who have believed in me when I didn't believe in myself and continually whisper (and sometimes shout) in my ear that I still have a story to tell.

And finally, to my four children who have shared their mother with India and who continually inspire me to do what I can to make the world a better place.

INTRODUCTION

I DID NOT KNOW . . .

I did not know what lay ahead when I boarded that plane bound for cyclone devastated rural villages in eastern India in November of 2000. Nor did I know how desperately my skills as a physical therapist specializing in pediatric burn care would be needed on that volunteer medical team. I had assumed that once this two-week trip was over I would get back to the very busy life of home schooling my four children; I would never again have anything to do with India. I couldn't have been more wrong.

I DID NOT KNOW . . .

I did not know how quickly I would shed my American comforts and fall head over heals in love the people of India. Although I am a water snob, a clean-air snob, and a bit of clean freak, the dirty water, air, and general filth didn't bother me. The Indian people mesmerized me. There were people everywhere I looked—people stuffed into small homes, packed into cars, trains, buses, and motorcycles. There were people swarming the sidewalks and pouring into the streets and I instantly connected with them.

I DID NOT KNOW . . .

I did not know that India is a vast country of 1.2 billion people divided into a hierarchical caste system. There are four main castes and a category called the outcaste. There are 250 million people in the outcaste who are, because of the karma of their past lives, relegated to the "dirty" jobs. They tan leather, butcher meat, pick up excrement (human and animal), sweep streets, and clean toilets. Because their jobs are literally dirty, the outcastes are considered too dirty to touch or be around—they are considered untouchable.

I DID NOT KNOW . . .

I did not know that I would not be able to get the plight of the Dalits out of my heart and mind. I started talking to everyone I knew about it. I wrote stories about my adventures while I was on the medical trip and passed out photographs of the people who so captured my heart. In the spring of 2001, a devastating earth quake hit the Indian state of Gujarat. I worked with a local non-profit to help send containers of medical supplies to the area. My church decided to get more involved in the recovery work so I headed up their effort and started a committee called Imagine India. Through the tireless efforts of those committee members, we put on a conference and brought the international Dalit expert Joseph D'souza to lecture to the attendees.

I DID NOT KNOW . . .

I did not know that all over North and South India Dalits were beginning a grassroots effort to leave the caste system. Dalits organized a rally convening over 100,000 Dalits from all over India. They came together in unity in November of 2001 to say that they no longer wanted to accept the oppression and abuse of the caste system – they wanted out – they wanted their freedom. Dalit leaders met with Christian leaders during that week and the coalition of hundreds agreed together that the best mechanism for the Dalits' freedom would be found in the education of their children. With of population of 250 million, lots and lots of quality English education schools would be necessary to see the emancipation of these people.

I DID NOT KNOW....

I did not know the significant need there was to tell the world about the plight of the Dalits. Dr. D'souza realized the enormity of this situation and decided that there needed to be an organization in the west that was fully devoted to the cause of the Dalits. They would be a group of people that would become the experts in the Dalit situation. Abolitionists around the world raising awareness, finances, and human resources to see this people group freed from the slavery that has defined their life. The Dalit Freedom Network (DFN) was born and I was appointed Executive Director.

I DID NOT KNOW....

I did not know how deeply rooted the racial and religious biases ran between sects of people. One year after the devastating earthquake in Gujarat, violent riots broke out between the Hindus and the Muslims. Thousands of Muslims were killed and over 100,000 were left homeless. Muslim homes and businesses had been burned to the ground and stories of horrible atrocities equal to the Rwanda genocide were leaking out to us in the states. I asked a couple of women to go to India on a research trip. They interviewed Indian women who had lived through the violent riots, recorded their stories, held their hands, and compiled it all into a report that was part of congressional testimony in the fall of 2002. The word was out that we will no longer idly sit by and watch the oppression and persecution of the outcasts of India.

I DID NOT KNOW....

I did not know how the efforts of so many people could create a movement that has a life of it's own. By 2003 we had our 501(c) 3 status, a foundation was paying for our development department, a partner organization funded staff salary, artists were getting involved and bringing their voice to the issue, the media was covering the topic, and thousands of people around the US began working for the emancipation of the Dalits of India.

Through the years I have had the privilege of traveling on medical, educational, or vision trips all over India. These are the photographs and stories of some of my experiences there. I hope they will open the eyes of your heart to the lost and forgotten nation of India. Enjoy the photographs and gain a new perspective of your own life from the stories.

SO NOW WE ALL CAN KNOW.................

WHITEWASHED LIVES AND REAL BLOOD

The slums of Calcutta were like nothing I have experienced before. It had rained quite a bit before we got there, and the mud and slime that coated everything contributed to the dreary, oppressed atmosphere. Finding a place to set up a temporary medical clinic is difficult when all the "houses" are stacked row after row after row with only three feet separating each row. Each of the homes in the slums are 10 by 10 structures made from plywood, sheet metal, or tarp. The national workers helping us finally found a space large enough for the clinic—it was available only because a trash dump rather than a building occupied it. The workers dug out trash for three days. Out of this space they "whitewashed" everything with bright and beautiful orange and white nylon cloth. They built a wood frame for the sides, top, and bottom. Then they completely covered the area—even the floor had canvas on it. From the inside of the clinic, you had no way of knowing you were in the middle of a very muddy slum. It was quite surreal. Just on the other side of my physical therapy room was a sweatshop where seamstresses sewed twelve hours a day on foot-powered machines. A peek through a hole in our nylon wall revealed a very gloomy work area with hard-working Dalits cranking out cheap clothing products for Americans.

Many other conditions in the slums were also "white washed." I treated patients all day long with much deeper problems than they at first appeared to have. There was a boy who had narrowly escaped a fire in his home and had somehow jammed a nail through his fingernail in the process. His finger was inflamed and swollen. It didn't look terrible, but I knew we needed to get below the surface to see what was really going on. After numbing the pain with an injection, I started to peel off layers of his skin and even took off the entire fingernail. The tissue below the surface was infected and dying, and if gone untreated could easily have killed him. It took a lot to clean off the top layer of dead and useless skin and get down to the real tissue. I had to cut and cut until the tissue bled—the sign that I had finally reached healthy tissue.

We saw another man whose daughter asked us to visit him in his home because he was very ill. The house was 10 square feet holding his 8-foot platform bed. This man could no longer walk. His abdomen was quite swollen and he had constant spasms that caused great pain to shoot through his body. We worked hard to figure out the history of his condition and what could possibly be wrong. We probably spent an hour discussing all his symptoms. It was so difficult because he desperately wanted us to help him and we couldn't. We prayed for him and finally left, telling him we would help pay for some investigative tests. Minutes later the man's brother showed up at the clinic with a host of tests that had already been done. He told us his brother actually had end stage cancer and that neither he nor the rest of his family knew about it.

WHITEWASHED.

COVERING UP THE PAIN.

NOT BEING TRUTHFUL WITH WHAT IS REALLY GOING ON INSIDE.

DEATH IS WAITING AT THE DOOR AND NO ONE IS FACING IT.

I GUESS THAT IS THE WAY TO SURVIVE IN SUCH BLEAK CIRCUMSTANCES. I GUESS IT MAKES IT EASIER TO DEAL WITH DEEP PAIN WHEN YOU CAN COVER IT UP WITH SOMETHING "PRETTIER." I THINK WE ALL DO THAT TO SOME EXTENT. HIDING HERE IN OUR BEAUTIFUL HOMES WITH PRETTY OUTSIDES, WE ARE OFTEN DYING INSIDE AND REFUSING TO FACE THE PAIN. WE HAVE WHAT LOOKS LIKE "HEALTHY" SKIN ON THE OUTSIDE WHILE THE TISSUE UNDERNEATH IS CANCEROUS AND DEAD. I think God calls us to a healthier life. HE WANTS US TO STRIP AWAY THAT FAKE EXTERIOR AND SCRAPE OFF THE DYING TISSUE UNTIL WE CAN BLEED, EXPOSING THE TISSUE BELOW THAT WANTS TO LIVE.

HOW WAS YOUR TRIP?

How do I answer people when I return from India and they want to know how my trip was? I don't have a concise response. Usually asking on the run, do they really want an answer? Even with all the time in the world, how could I describe the India that I know and love?

The logistics are simple enough to explain: Our team of thirty hold medical clinics in rural villages throughout India. We treat over 7,500 patients each trip. I see people with cerebral palsy, arthritis, genetic deformities, neck and back pain, untreated diabetes, unset old fractures, infected open wounds, polio, and leprosy. I spend days in small, crowded rooms with a translator by my side giving exercises to patients, creating splints, casts and shoe lifts, and cleaning infected wounds.

We keep a tight schedule and work furiously each day, perhaps stopping for a lunch break and a walk through the village, until we leave the clinic for the hotel. The short evenings are filled with pre-ordered dinners we share together and time to process our day before repacking our medical supplies and finally laying down to sleep.

While the logistics merely explain what we did—they cannot convey an understanding of our experience. The trips are simply not about numbers, diagnoses, or schedules. They are about people and the lost and forgotten nation of India. They are not the media's perception of the new booming Indian economy and luxury lifestyles, but the real India. It's about the India that 80% of its population experiences. The trips are about walking through a village and having a family rush out to invite me into their house for chai. It's about looking into the face of a woman my age and wondering at the life experiences that make her appear twice as old.

It's about trying to enter their world, if only for a moment. Sharing life with them and trying to ease their burden, if only for a moment. It's about hearing health complaints all day and working to solve them, yet understanding that their deepest struggle is inside their soul.

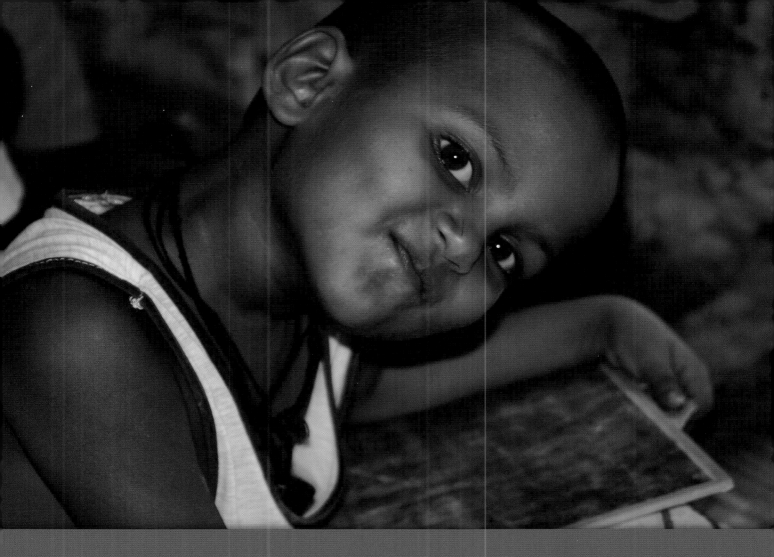

It's about working with a great team of people from many backgrounds united for an important cause—the common good of humankind. American, Czech, Scottish, and Indian Christians, Muslims, and Hindus joined with respect and encouragement for one another, living out of love. The real value of the trips lies in relationships. Relationships with a team of diverse nationalities and relationships with the villagers we serve. True faith calls us to live such a life of love and relationships.

The lessons from these experiences sometimes go deeper than words can express; they stir in my spirit and settle there. God has spoken to me in ways that transcend short anecdotes and will stay with me forever. In some trips, God miraculously reveals himself to me many times each day. In other trips, I experience his steady presence in less dramatic forms and I understand all over again his power, goodness and sovereignty. I reawake afresh to His grace, mercy, and love for me and the nation of India. In a powerful way I cannot explain, I hear again His call to intertwine my life with the beautiful people of India.

So how do I wrap that up in a pretty summary to explain to others in a hurry?

CREATION TESTIFIES

We all have anchors that get us through each day. The rhythm of our schedules, the activities of our families, performing well at work, or even the rituals of mealtime can all be anchors. They are the routines that provide stability and grounding for us. The character of God in creation is an anchor for me. Each morning I marvel at the splendor of the sunrise and remember that His mercies are new every morning. I look to the mountains and know that he is my Rock—never changing—never leaving me—never forsaking. With each sunset I marvel at His magnificent creativity and beauty. Each day is accompanied by a running conversation with God as he draws my attention to Himself through His creation.

In the slums of Calcutta, I feel assaulted by a brutal separation from any evidence of God's creation......   ......outside of the humans living there.

The entire place is covered in a thin, bleak mud. The plywood homes huddle together so closely I can barely see the sky. I walk through the narrow pathways and begin to panic, wondering where it all ends and how to get out. Nothing grows here, no trees, no bushes, no grasses, and no vegetables. There are no birds, no insects, and no animals. The sprawling slum is desolate of anything but humans and the structures that provide barely enough shelter for life. Except for the girls and boys, men and women who live there every day, all I see is plywood, sheet metal walls, metal pots, clothes drying everywhere, and dirty gray structures......

There is nothing here that God created......   ......except for the humans.

I grope to remind myself of God's presence in the slums and I realize I must hope to see Him in the people surrounding me. Somehow, though it is easier to see Him in the majestic Rocky Mountains than in the frustrated woman beside me. I thank God daily for the inanimate and animal creations that testify to His character. Less often do I thank God for the various people around me—certainly not for the aggravating ones.

I rarely see beauty in the qualities of people whom are difficult to be around. I don't often praise God for the character growth that comes from dealing with them. If I lived in the slums, could I learn to find the beauty in every human God created there? Would they become my anchors be to get me through each day?

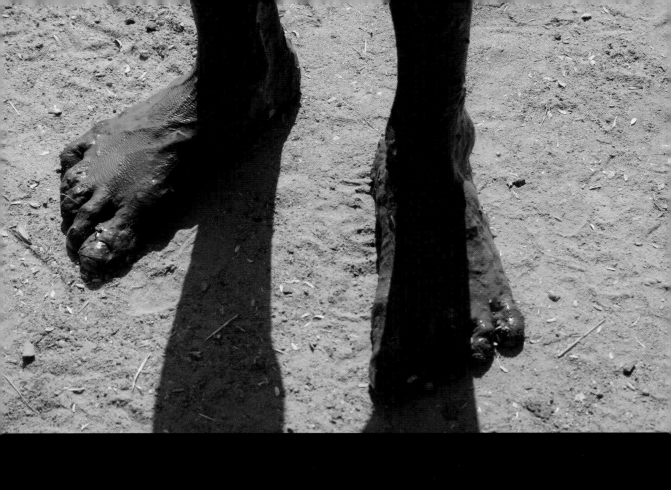

BEAUTIFUL FEET

My dad owned and managed a shoe store. My grandfather and great grandfather did too. It was a family business, a town's family store where everyone could go and find a pair of shoes. I worked there one summer and loved it. All three of my brothers worked there through out high school. It was a family business we were all proud of. It was fun to help people find the shoe they wanted/needed and serve them. We were taught to size their feet, place the shoe on their feet and make sure "the shoe fit". Feet have always been a fascination to me. I photograph them in all sorts of ways. I like to massage them and I am always noticing the peculiarities of other people's feet.

Feet mean something entirely different in India. They are considered quite offensive. I remember having an Indian anatomy professor in college that yelled and publicly humiliated one of my classmates because his feet were up on the chair and pointing at the professor. Feet are an insult – dirty – unclean – and they represent the station in life of half the population. The caste sytem is divided up based on where that particular caste is placed on the gods body. The Sudhras (low caste) are the caste of people that come from the feet. The Dalits (untouchables) are even lower than the Sudhras, not even originating from gods body, and most of them go barefoot or wear thin flip-flops. If the Dalits are walking through a higher caste part of a village, they will have to remove their shoes to walk through that section of the village because their shoes walking in that part of the village would make it unclean.

The Dalits are the "shoe men" of India. Because shoes are made out of leather, and leather comes from tanning the skin from a dead animal; the "leatherworkers" are Dalit. You see the caste system is based on a person's profession, and all the professions that work with "dirty" things are relegated to the outcastes, the untouchables, the Dalits. They butcher meat, tan leather, sweep streets, cremate bodies, pick up human and animal excrement: all the jobs that are unclean. Just "above" the Dalits are the Sudhra's or the low caste – they come from the feet of the god's body.

I can't imagine identifying myself with a part of the body that everyone hated. How damaging to my soul would it be to look at a foot and think how horrible and unclean it is, and then to subconsciously think the same about myself. In my work I have come to know and respect a beautiful Dalit woman activist. She has sacrificed much of her life so she can be a voice for the poor and oppressed in India. She walks miles and miles stirring up a grassroots social justice effort. A couple years ago I was involved in a ceremony where Christian leaders apologized to other religious leaders for past disharmony. Part of the ceremony included a time to wash the feet of the other leaders in a show of servant solidarity for them. I was asked to wash the feet of my activist friend. As she came up on stage and realized what was about to happen, she automatically protested and would not let me touch her feet. I told her how much I respected her. I told her I am so grateful for her work and want her to know that. I told her I want to work humbly alongside her in this effort. That washing her feet is a symbol of my solidarity to her.

AS I KNELT IN FRONT OF HER AT HER FEET, SHE CONTINUED TO REFUSE STATING HER FEET ARE HORRIBLE AND I WOULD NOT WANT TO TOUCH THEM. SHE IS A DALIT — RESIDING BELOW THE FEET IN THE CASTE HIERARCHY. WHAT ARE HER INTERNAL VOICES SAYING TO HER ABOUT HER OWN SELF WORTH.

MY DAD, GRANDFATHER, AND GREAT GRANDFATHER WERE ALL "SHOEMEN".

If I lived in India I would be Dalit.

Naked and Unashamed

I visited a village just outside Chennai to see if it was a good place to build a school for Dalit children. When we first drove up to the village, it looked nearly abandoned. A local woman leader excitedly grabbed me by the hand and started screaming for all the women and children to come out of their homes. Dozens and dozens of lovely, dirty, half-dressed, screaming children piled all around me. The woman talked wildly about the future of her people—how all of the children needed an education and that there was no hope for their village without empowering the next generation. I wondered if I could hire her to write brochures for our office!

The fact that these children were home during the day, dirty, and not fully clothed spoke volumes to me about the poverty of this village. If they had the resources, these children would have been clean, dressed, and in school instead of home working to put food in their stomachs.

I asked if I could photograph the beautiful children to remember my experience and her village. The woman began to grab children and push them in front of my camera. Through my lens, I noticed a quiet girl, maybe 11 or 12 years old. She was all but naked – her torn, very small underpants were her only covering. Her developing breasts lay exposed. Even so, the girl had tied a colorful scarf around her neck. Hiding none of her nakedness, she expressed her desire to be beautiful. I was fascinated.

I don't know when it happens, but at some point, most of us become ashamed of nakedness.-certainly not when we are toddlers. When my children were just learning to walk, they loved to run free without diapers, completely naked. The adoring photographs I took of them are so cute in the family photo album. My children now scream, horrified, when they see these—to think that I would dare show off a picture of their two-year-old selves completely naked! Psychologists tell us that this developed sense of shame of our naked body is normal and theologians tell us our shame has been around since the fall in the Garden of Eden.

I wondered whether this girl had any respect for her body to understand that she needed to be clothed, and yet she wanted that colorful scarf wrapped around her neck. Was she too poor to have any clothes or was she just so socially malnourished she didn't understand she needed clothes? I wanted to protect her and yet give her freedom all at the same time.

It grieves me to think about all the girls in India who do not know they deserve dignity and respect. How tragic it is that millions of women worldwide have healthy and unhealthy shame all twisted up, entangling them.

How sad to think that for a number of reasons, this girl will never blush at her naked picture in a family photo album.

LIVING ON A GOLD MINE

"What do I have in my hand?" I don't know where I first heard this expression. I think it came from a talk at MOPS when a woman spoke about not going to the grocery everyday for food but instead to look at what you already have in your kitchen and use those ingredients. Substitute honey for sugar, use parsley instead of cilantro, make a salad instead of stir-frying veggies. With four small children, I quickly learned to apply this concept to all kinds of systems in my home. I used it to teach my children flexibility and problem-solving skills as I home schooled them. It's surprising how much we have "in our hands" if we look closely enough.

When I had the opportunity to visit the minefields in southern India to see the abject poverty of these residents, the thought that ran through my mind was, "What do they have in their hand? They are living on a goldmine." This is another figure of speech we use in the States to talk about people who own a house on top of land that is worth a lot. It implies that people can have something of great value and not be able to "monetize" it. Living on "gold mine" properties can be great if you can figure out how to truly capitalize on the resources you "hold."

The Dalits in these minefields had lost their ability to capitalize on the gold mines beneath their feet. Just five years ago, they thrived by working in the mines hiding kilometers below their modest homes. Then the corruption that is so common to India ruined their lives. So many "bosses" were taking their share of the profit that it actually cost the government more to get the gold out of the ground than they could make selling it. With gold prices as high as they are these days, that's a sobering fact.

Consequently, this community of tens of thousands of people has become completely disenfranchised and disengaged from each other. Husbands and wives leave their homes early in the morning and take a train into Bangalore to work all day for a dollar or two. They leave their children to fend for themselves back in the village for twelve hours every day, some as young as two or three years old.

As I walked through the village, I caught a glimpse of life without adult supervision. Toddlers roamed around with tears in their eyes and no one to comfort them or meet their most basic physical needs. Ten-year olds worked hard to collect water, wash clothes on rocks, and boil up pots of rice for lunch. Some children just ran amuck to taunt and hurt whomever they pleased. I know their parents didn't want to leave their children unattended all day long, but what else could they do when the only possible work lay two hours away?

I met with local leaders and heard the same plea from each, "Please help us find another economy to help us support ourselves." They were not asking for a handout: they didn't think the Americans had come to solve their problems. They just wanted help redefining their lives—to look at what they had in their hands that could turn into work.

As a result, we started training programs to teach them to be tailors, repair bicycles, and iron clothes for a living. We also started a school to give their children the much-desired English education that would enable them to find good jobs in the future. Even though they literally were living on a gold mine, they found other means to live.

We helped them find other ways to live with dignity and respect, and to discover that the true resource they had in their hands was their humanity.

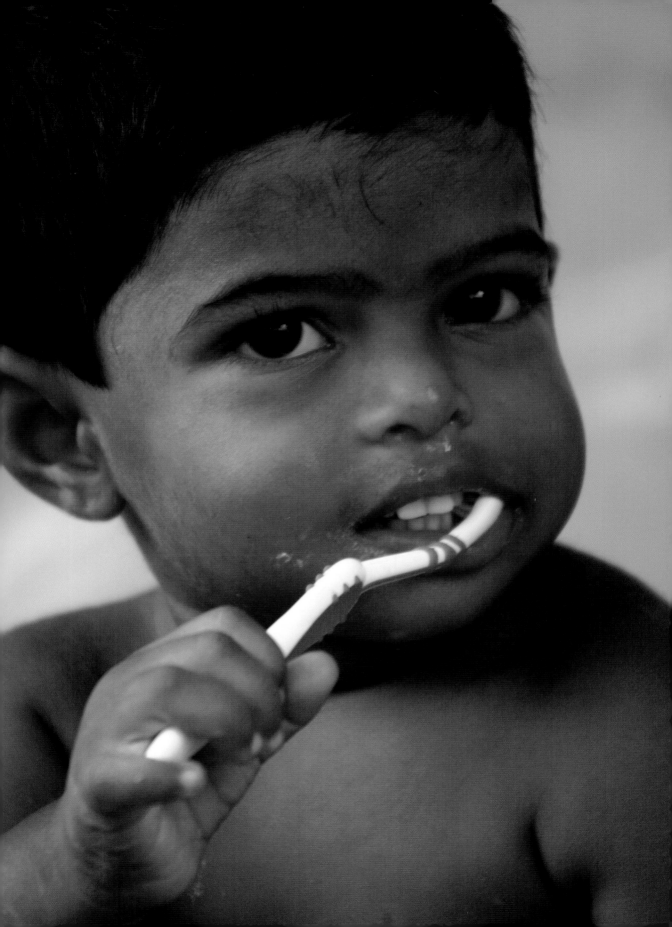

IMPORTANT PEOPLE

The medical trip to India after the tsunami was particularly difficult. I often think that when the tsunami hit Asia it also hit me. What we saw on the ground and the stories we heard will impact me forever. What I learned of human nature still haunts and yet teaches me.

I was particularly tense one day. We had just arrived at this village and asked the leaders how many people had died. The village leader reported losing 350 people and 100 Dalits. As if the Dalits were not part of the human race.

Those words still whirl around in my head.

In fact, the tsunami had killed so many adults in this village that dozens upon dozens of children instantly became orphans. The District Collector (the county "mayor") had decided this particular village needed playground equipment to help the children forget their grief—a good idea in theory but not well thought through. Besides the fact that what the children really needed was emotional and psychological support, the playground equipment was not safe. I treated children with injuries from the new playground all day long. My very first patient was a little boy who fractured his arm sliding down the slide. It was so steep the kids barreled down too fast and crashed at the bottom. They did finally devise a way to not hurt themselves—by holding onto each other to form a train they only had to career down the last bit of the slide.

The day grew late and I still had twenty patients to treat when someone interrupted my work, asking me to meet "a very important person." I was quite sure the very important people were right there in the clinic waiting to be treated, but I went anyway. It was the District Collector who had come to observe our work. I walked after him as he inspected each of the clinic rooms and told him about the medical personnel on the team and the types of patients we had treated so far.

When he no longer needed me, I hurried back to the clinic but was stopped by a reporter who wanted to do a television interview. I expected questions about the loss in the village and the types of injuries we had seen. Instead, this woman wanted to hear about the playground. She wanted me to confirm that the gift was great and the village was thrilled to have it. I pictured the steady stream of children I had seen today who were injured by that equipment and I didn't exactly believe the playground would help ease the orphans' feelings of loss. So, I did not comply with her questions—they only made me angrier at the lack of true understanding people had regarding the needs of these children.

After the interview, I stormed back to my clinic where I was again interrupted in order to meet more "important people." The whole concept of important and unimportant people had become a source of anger for me and I almost turned down the request. Fortunately, I decided to greet the visitors because I met two Dalit leaders who lived nearby. They had collected money from the Dalits in their district to give to the other Dalits affected by the tsunami.

Wow. What a privilege to meet these two men! What an honor that they came to us and entrusted us with their hard-earned donations because they knew we understood how to help the Dalits. What a contrast to the District Collector who haphazardly gave government money to an easy project that avoided the root of the problem. These men made sacrifices and earnestly sought to serve their suffering brothers and sisters. In my mind, these were the important people.

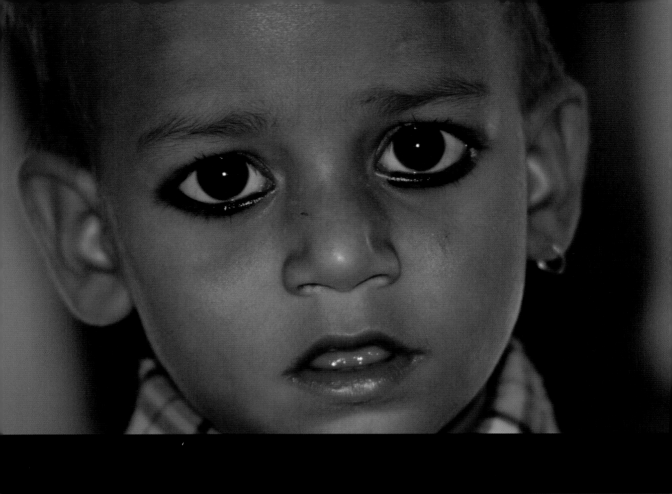

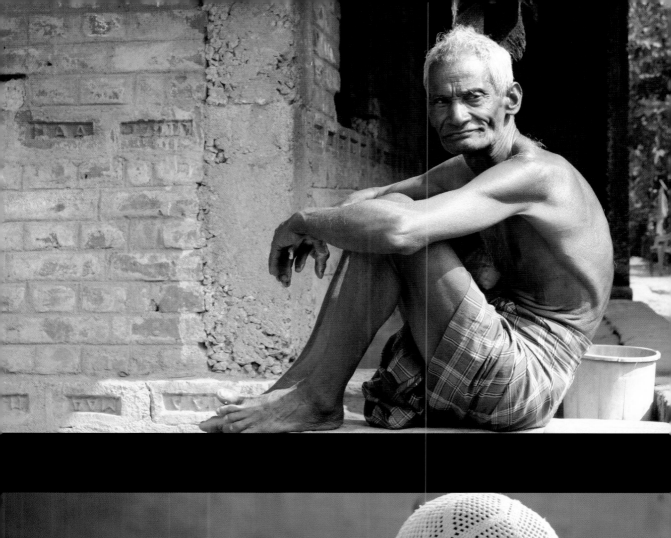

HEAVY LOAD

I love showers. On a cold winter's night, warm water pounding my body rivals a warm blanket and hot tea. Like comfort food, a warm shower centers my soul for the day. I can do my best thinking in the shower, but I'm a "green" kind of person and feel guilty about wasting water. Sinking into the comfort of the shower, I quickly remember that I am letting precious resources run down the drain at my feet. Comforting or not, I need to shut the water off and get on with my day.

The 2004 tsunami left much of India with severe water shortages. By the time our medical team arrived just three weeks after the disaster, villagers faced restricted supplies. Relief agencies had placed large water tanks in the villages so Indian water trucks could fill them each morning. Some villages had pumps that opened like a fire hydrant for only thirty minutes each morning. Each family in the village had to collect their day's water in a few minutes from that one pump.

Restricted as this was, it still appeared to be a decent system, but then Dalit villagers told me they couldn't get clean water. I looked at the nearby water tank, confused. They explained that the water trucks refused to fill the tanks on the Dalit side of the village. The truck drivers would not "dirty" themselves by entering the Dalits' area. In villages with pumps, the Dalit could only watch the water flow from a distance. Touching the pumps would taint the supply and make everything "unclean."

ONE DAY, I SAW THIS LITTLE GIRL MAKING THE BEST OF THE WATER SHORTAGES AND DISCRIMINATION. THE PUMP WAS OPEN AND SHE WAS "HELPING" HER MOTHER FILL THE JUGS. WHEN HER MOTHER CARRIED TWO FULL JARS BACK TO THE HOUSE, THE GIRL WENT TO WORK ON THE REMAINING JUGS. SHE QUICKLY FILLED ONE UP AND STRUGGLED TO FILL THE SECOND. The first jug was too heavy for her to move and if the second jug went on top of the first, the water missed the opening. THE GIRL FINALLY FILLED THE SECOND JUG, PICKED IT UP, AND STARTED TOWARDS HOME. SHE QUICKLY DISCOVERED IT WAS FAR TOO HEAVY TO CARRY FILLED WITH WATER, SO SHE MADE AN EXECUTIVE DECISION TO DUMP THE WATER AND CARRY THE JUG BACK TO HER MOTHER EMPTY. AFTER ALL, IT WAS SO MUCH EASIER TO CARRY WITHOUT ALL THAT WATER WEIGHING IT DOWN. I LAUGHED SO HARD I HAD TO STOP TAKING PHOTOGRAPHS OF HER DILEMMA.

I can't fault her wasting the water. I do it daily at home in my own shower—I don't often think about my part in the grand scheme of preserving the Earth's resources either. The problem for her was that she didn't understand the big picture of her mother's intended accomplishment.

IN OUR FINITE MINDS, EMPTYING OUR FULL WATER JUGS IN ORDER TO CARRY A LIGHTER LOAD MAKES PERFECT SENSE. MAYBE THOUGH, WE OUGHT TO KEEP THE WATER IN THE JUG AND CARRY THE HEAVY LOAD ALL THE WAY HOME TO FULFILL God's Grand Scheme of life.

NESTING

In America, most of us sit in front of the television to watch other people on the news endure tragedy. Some of us join relief efforts to try to help, but few of us experience tragedy directly. **Until you live through a disaster, I don't think you can predict your reaction.**

When our medical team first landed in India three weeks after the 2004 tsunami hit, we had no idea what to expect. We didn't know if we would help locate dead bodies, spend most of our time counseling, or treat a myriad of open wounds and compound fractures.

As we loaded the bus on our first morning, someone told us there were other Americans here and asked if we wanted to meet them? With the team already on the bus, I hurried to meet a gentleman who traveled from the US to help the relief efforts. **He was indignant about how the Indians were reacting to the trauma.** He said they just sat around waiting for others to help them. All he could see were piles of trash and hundreds of people just sitting, staring into the distance.

I got defensive for the villagers in the beautiful country I had come to love. I finally stood up and

said "I guess you and I have no way of knowing how we would react if our entire world had just disappeared under a wall of water." I quickly excused myself and jumped on the bus.

On the road to the medical clinic, a whole village of people ran out and waved at us to stop. Their temporary tents, food rations, and new clothes showed that a well-known international relief organization had already helped them. Why where they so insistent that we stop? The leaders took me on a long walk and showed me a thorough inventory of all the things they had lost: Their boat motors were lined up in an orderly row, the cracked and broken skiffs sat neatly categorized on the beach, the tangled clumps of fishing nets lay piled beside the road.

I saw an elderly woman slowly drag the remnants of her shattered home and possessions to the place where her house once stood. That house was now a pile of trash that she stacked on her land. I watched, fascinated. She reminded me of a woman nesting right before giving birth—organizing her home with an attention to detail she never had before, like cleaning the corners of every room with a toothbrush—an instinctual response to imminent and sudden change. I thought it interesting that the nesting response kicked in after almost total loss and not only before joyful gain.

WE WANTED TO HELP THIS VILLAGE BUT DIDN'T KNOW HOW. WHAT THEY REALLY WANTED WAS OUR VOICE. THEY WERE EAGER TO RETURN TO THEIR LIVELIHOOD, TO THE OCEAN, BUT THE GOVERNMENT HAD NOT REIMBURSED THEM FOR THE LOST BOATS, NETS, AND MOTORS AS PROMISED. THEY DIDN'T WANT MORE HANDOUTS; THEY WANTED THE ABILITY TO FISH AND MAKE AN HONEST LIVING FOR THEIR FAMILIES. THEY WANTED TO CONTINUE WITH THE PROFESSIONS THAT GAVE THEIR LIVES RHYTHM, MEANING, AND PURPOSE.

THEY ASKED IF WE WOULD PROMPT THE AUTHORITIES TO SEND THE SETTLEMENTS QUICKLY. The villagers had no voice—they were Dalits and Sudhras, and they were ignored, BUT THEY BELIEVED THE GOVERNMENT WOULD LISTEN TO OUR AMERICAN VOICES INSTEAD.

THE VILLAGERS WANTED QUICK ACTION. THEY HELD A DEEP SENSE THAT RETURNING TO WORK WAS THE HEALTHIEST RESPONSE. WHAT ONE PERSON SAW AS PILES OF TRASH AND PEOPLE WAITING TO BE RESCUED WAS ACTUALLY A GROUP OF PEOPLE INSTINCTIVELY RESPONDING TO TRAUMA, trying to move forward and rebuild their lives.

POLAR OPPOSITES

Sometimes I wonder what road I'm on. I want to change the world. I want to eliminate caste-based discrimination and improve the life situation for the Dalits. But sometimes I don't know if that's what I'm doing, because in the complex work of relief and development, reality is never as it appears.

As our medical team worked in the tsunami devastated villages along the Indian coast, one of our Indian partners asked me to take a break and visit a village of Dalits two miles inland who survived by raising pigs. I was not prepared for what I saw there—the conditions were the worst I had seen in all of India. The people lived in huts with only two or three walls of tree leaves and flimsy wood. These meager homes were arranged around the village's economic and social center: the pigsty.

The children of the village played, as all children do, except these children, at least those younger than twelve, were naked and they played with the pigs in the mud of the sty.

I saw one small boy, maybe two-years old, lying on his back. He did not swat the flies that covered him and his bloated belly made him look nine months pregnant. He was starving to death. I turned to the village leaders who began to tell me their devastating story.

Each night, higher-caste men get drunk at a nearby bar and raid the Dalit village, raping the women and girls. Any Dalit who complained was beaten or killed.

My Western view of the world makes it difficult to understand how the "untouchables," who supposedly contaminate others on contact, can be raped with impunity.

Adding to this nightly torment, the recent tsunami had ruined them as completely as the costal villages even though the village was never underwater. Their source of income had dried up as the coastal villages got their food from relief agencies and no longer needed to buy pigs. The leaders explained to me that they could not kill and eat their own pigs—for a day's worth of meat, they would forfeit a profit that could feed them for a month.

This village of several hundred Dalits was ignored—forgotten—by the rest of the world. They waited and hoped that the coast would need their pigs again, and that life would improve.

Overwhelmed and desperate to help, I asked the leaders, "If you could have one thing in the world, what would it be?" I was ready to give clothing for the naked children and food for the starving boy. Surely too, the men would seek justice for their wives and daughters.

Instead, they responded in unison: "WATER."

Twenty feet away stood a hand pump that pulled clean water from the ground, but these villagers could not use it because they are Dalit. Any contact with the well would "taint" the water supply. Attempts to access this water brought beatings, more rapes, and threats of death. So, they were forced to walk for miles on public roads they were not "allowed" to use to draw water from a polluted monsoon pond.

AS THE PRESIDENT OF THE DALIT FREEDOM NETWORK, I THOUGHT SURELY I COULD DO SOMETHING TO HELP THIS VOICELESS DALIT VILLAGE. WHEN THEY POINTED TO THE WATER, MY SPIRITS FELL AS I REALIZED HOW UNBELIEVABLY CONVOLUTED WAS THIS MESS: THE ONE THING THEY WANTED MORE THAN ANYTHING WAS RIGHT IN FRONT OF THEM, INACCESSIBLE, AND NOT FOR LACK OF TECHNOLOGY OR RESOURCES, BUT BECAUSE OF HUMAN DEPRAVITY AND ABSURD DISCRIMINATION.

WITHIN A WEEK OF MY VISIT, I WAS IN AN EVENING GOWN AND PEARLS IN WASHINGTON, DC WITH A PLATE OF PRIME RIB AND ASPARAGUS IN FRONT OF ME THAT I KNEW I WOULDN'T BE ABLE TO FINISH. WITH THOUGHTS OF THE STARVING BOY FROM THE PIG VILLAGE, I EXCUSED MYSELF FROM THE TABLE AND RUSHED TO BATHROOM TO GAIN SOME COMPOSURE. HOW COULD I SIT HERE IN SUCH WASTEFUL ELEGANCE? How could I reconcile the unbelievably opposing life circumstances between the pig village and my life? AT THAT MOMENT, I KNOW GOD TOLD ME THAT OUR EFFORTS IN WASHINGTON WOULD HELP THOSE PEOPLE 12,000 MILES AWAY, THAT IT DOES MATTER—A DIFFERENCE WILL BE MADE. GOD, I BELIEVE IT WILL. HELP ME WITH MY UNBELIEF.

SAFETY ON THE BRIDGE

Cri-sis: (noun) *a time of intense difficulty, trouble, or danger*

When people go through a crisis sometimes they will find an inanimate object that brings them comfort—a favorite blanket, a teddy bear or pillow, food, a television program, a letter from a family member or a loved article of clothing. The connection can be made on why that object comforts them, but in reality, the object itself brings more comfort to the person than the power it really has to protect or comfort.

Nothing could be more true than when I spent a few days with a village in India that survived the tsunami. Three weeks after the devastating tsunami of 2004, as my medical relief team continued its efforts, we arrived in what I call the "bridge village." A short drive south of Chennai, the bridge village sits next to the Indian Ocean at the mouth of a river. The Indian government had worked for seven years to complete a skinny one kilometer-long bridge over the river that nearly surrounds the village before flowing into the sea. Months after the completion of the bridge, the tsunami struck and the village was flooded in minutes. Bordered by the ocean and the river, the only villagers to survive were the ones who made it to the safety of the bridge.

When our medical team arrived a few weeks later, the villagers were just feeling safe enough to leave the safety of the bridge and return to their homes. At the end of our second day there, the local officials received a disturbing phone call. Police from Chennai called for the immediate evacuation of the village. The officials feared that a recent earthquake, full moon, and high tide had made the perfect conditions for another tsunami.

This was horrific news to the poor villagers who had just begun to recover from the trauma of the tsunami. Pandemonium erupted as hundreds of villagers panicked. Screaming, fainting, they threw their children at us, as if our US citizenship could save them. Old men carried their fragile wives, others dragged fainted women by their feet. The entire village clamored to the three-foot wide stairs that led to safety on top of the bridge.

Our Indian partners screamed for us to climb to safety too. I struggled to figure out what was happening. I was sure it was impossible for another tsunami to hit this exact village again so soon. Statistically it just could not happen. My team members were confused and unsure of how to react. All of us were saddened as we watched the villagers become traumatized all over again. What should we do? How should we react?

I sure didn't want to push my way up the stairs in front of any villagers, but I did need to think about the safety of the team if in fact there could be flooding. So we all climbed the stairs, calmly trying to comfort people along the way.

We spent an hour or two on top of the bridge until our medical team finally gathered in vehicles and drove away. We drove away…. while all the villagers still camped out on top of the bridge. Away from the people we had traveled so far to comfort and care for, left behind in their fear and confusion. Another tsunami did not happen that day and we returned a few days later to hand out relief supplies—our attempt to calm them and ease their fear. Several months later, after we left the village did flood again. Unexplainably.

Once again, the villagers found solace in the safety of the bridge. The bridge had become their inanimate object of safety and it makes me wonder - where do I go for comfort when I am faced with a crisis? Where are my bridges that provide safety?

Ocean Swim

Anytime I am near water I have this uncontrollable desire to jump in and swim around. Water draws me to itself. Lakes, pools, the ocean, they beckon me to dive in and float free amidst all that life. I could swim almost anywhere and stay in for hours, but I'm also a bit afraid of the water, particularly the ocean. Unknown creatures and the incomprehensible force in waves share my common space as I swim in an environment that could kill me.

One of the villages our medical team visited after the tsunami used to be located mere yards from the oceanfront. We arrived to see the absurdity of makeshift tents "homes" crowded right next to the road while a mile of empty land stretches between the people and the coast. As we got out of the cars, the village leaders met us and immediately began to tell us their story.

For centuries they had fished the ocean, living just yards from high tide. Each morning the men went out to fish while their wives and children waited on the beach for them to bring in their catches. Then the women took the fish to market while the men rowed back out to catch more.

The ocean fed and sustained them and they worshiped it.

Then, unexpectedly, the ocean rose up in anger. They never knew the water contained such fury. They didn't know what they had done wrong or why the ocean god had punished them. Now they clearly feared the ocean's violent potential and they shunned the terror in it. And who could blame them? Several counselors had tried to walk along the coastline with villagers to lessen their fear of the water, but their attempts had been unsuccessful.

In another attempt to lessen the villagers' fear of the ocean, our medical team decided to go for a swim one very, very hot day after the clinic. I finished with patients early to make sure I could go, and at four in the afternoon we gathered the confident swimmers and struck out for the shore. Twenty feet from the water we ran as fast as we could and jumped into the waves with all our clothes on. We body surfed, dunked each other, and splashed about like children. It was a blast.

THE VILLAGERS CAME DOWN TO THE SHORE TO WATCH. WE BEGAN TO PLOT HOW TO "ENCOURAGE" OTHER TEAM MEMBERS INTO THE WATER. A FEW OF THE INDIAN TEAM MEMBERS GOT IN (SOME WITH OUR "HELP"). THEN ONE AND THEN TWO OF THE VILLAGERS GOT IN TOO. THEY WERE JUST KNEE DEEP, BUT THEY WERE WET FROM THE OCEAN FOR THE FIRST TIME SINCE THE TSUNAMI.

Breakthrough.

SOMETIMES WE THINK WE CAN HELP THE MOST BY PROVIDING MEDICAL CARE. SOMETIMES THE BEST THING WE CAN DO THOUGH IS SIMPLY TO LIVE OUR LIVES FEARLESSLY WITH GUSTO AND JOY.

JUSTICE

If there is one thing I want my children to understand and appreciate about the United States, it is our system of protection and justice. It's a difficult concept to impart to them—one that most adult Americans don't fully appreciate. It's the silent checks and balances that are in motion every minute of the day insuring that we can live our lives with the 299,999,999 other people in this country in relative peace, harmony, and freedom. It's even more difficult for me to explain to them why this doesn't automatically happen for the 250,000,000 Dalits in India, the world's largest democracy.

During one of our medical clinics, the Dalits were demonstrating against the government. They had lost absolutely everything in the tsunami—homes, possessions, loved ones— and had received no help from the government. The high-caste of the village, however, had already cashed their government checks to cover the water damage to their sturdy concrete homes. Apparently, the Dalits did not deserve humane treatment—most did not have an ID card so they did not "officially" exist in the eyes of the government.

I walked around the demonstration taking photographs and noticed a woman in a government jeep in the center of the crowd. She had driven down from Chennai to hear their complaints, but would not get out of her jeep to have a real conversation with the Dalits. The crowd was in the center of what used to be their neighborhood, but now it was just open, sandy land with no sign of their former homes—just unrecognizable, broken personal belongings, tangled fishnets, and pieces of shattered fishing boats.

After the lady in the jeep drove away, the crowd dispersed and I took more photographs of the desolate beach. As I rounded a corner there was a small group of Dalits obviously distressed and discussing something. One lady was squatting on the ground wringing her hands. I asked a tall gentleman in the group what was happening. He explained that they were waiting for the higher caste of the village to come and beat them for complaining to the government. My immediate reaction was to blurt out, "No way—they won't beat you for complaining." But he showed me stitches on his left ear and explained that last week they had complained about not getting relief food—in retaliation he had been hit with a bat, slicing open his ear. The woman on the ground was his mother, and he was trying to protect her from the imminent abuse.

JUSTICE. I DON'T KNOW HOW TO EXPLAIN TO MY CHILDREN THAT EVEN THOUGH THE LAWS OF INDIA PROTECT THE DALITS, IN REALITY THEY ARE SLAVES IN A SYSTEM THAT DAILY OPPRESSES AND ABUSES THEM – THAT EVEN THOUGH MANUAL SCAVENGING (CLEANING UP HUMAN EXCREMENT) IS OUTLAWED IN THE INDIAN CONSTITUTION, THERE ARE NEARLY A MILLION MANUAL SCAVENGERS THAT ARE EMPLOYED BY THE INDIAN GOVERNMENT. THAT DALIT WOMEN WHO ARE RAPED DON'T UNDERSTAND THEY HAVE A RIGHT TO FILE A CASE WITH THE POLICE WITHOUT GETTING RAPED AGAIN BY THEM. THE DAILY—HOURLY!— abuses to the Dalits in India baffle American minds BECAUSE WE TRUST A SYSTEM OF PROTECTION AND JUSTICE THAT SHOULD AUTOMATICALLY WORK.

And in the U.S. it mostly does.

DENIAL

ad-ap-ta-tion: (noun) *a change in which an organism or species becomes better suited to it's environment*

Humans have the amazing physical, psychological, and emotional capability to adapt to change. These adaptations can help us grow stronger and healthier in all areas of our lives. If we somehow block that growth, then our adaptations can become destructive. I see evidence of this every time I visit India.

The wound care segment of our Medical Clinic was extremely busy with wounds the tsunami gashed into its victims. The wounds were about three weeks old, completely untreated and festering. I flew through patients, working as fast as I could. Glancing at those waiting outside, I saw a man dressed in a clean, white Punjabi and surrounded by flies. The others in line kept their distance.

When the man walked in, he told me he had a problem with his foot. I'd seen enough leprosy patients to recognize this. What they perceive is never the disease, only a symptom.

I asked him to lie down and I cut off the rag bandage from his heel. Maggots burst out of the wound gasping at the new air. Fellow medical workers screamed or contained groans. I began to pick out the wormy creatures one, two, three at a time. As soon as I removed a few, more appeared in the wound. The wound cavity was so deep I could see through to the top of his foot.

I cleaned the wound, which the maggots had actually kept quite clean. Using donated materials— the best wound care products in the world—I packed his foot cavity, dressed his foot tightly to keep the maggots out, and asked him to return in a few days.

Later that week, I saw a cloud of flies in the clinic line surrounding the man in the white Punjabi. I cut the bandage and stripped away the expensive dressings. Once again, maggots burst forth.

I asked the man to sit up so we could talk face-to-face. Through the interpreter, I told him that he had leprosy. I told him he needed to go to a leprosarium to have his foot amputated.

Leprosy is a death sentence in India. Everyone knows it.

The man looked at me and said, no, he didn't have leprosy; he didn't have a wound on his foot, that it didn't even hurt. He assured me everything was okay. I got an old mirror and tried to show him the wound, but he said he couldn't see it because the mirror was cloudy and his eyes were bad. He insisted he was fine and he refused to be treated.

Weeks later, I couldn't stop dreaming about it. **Maggots don't belong inside a person.** They were slowly eating him, hiding in his increasingly numb nerve pathways. He needed drastic treatment, but he didn't grasp the severity of this disease—he couldn't feel it, so it must not exist.

AREN'T WE ALL NUMB TO SPIRITUAL MAGGOTS EATING US? WE DON'T ACKNOWLEDGE THE DEEP UNHEALTHINESS IN OUR CORE. WE IGNORE IT AND LET IT EAT AWAY AT OUR SOUL, WHEN WHAT WE REALLY NEED IS AN AMPUTATION. We fool ourselves into believing that the disturbing cloud of flies buzzing around us is unimportant THAT WE ARE JUST FINE. WHAT IF WE ADMITTED OUR DISEASE AND REALIZED THAT SAVING FACE IN THE SHORT-TERM CANNOT COMPARE TO THE BEAUTY OF FINDING TRUE, DEEP PEACE?

HOPE

Research shows that the people who survived the holocaust shared a common value: They believed their life mattered. If they thought they had a reason to exist, even if the reason was simply that they had a garden to tend, they survived. As we've seen before, you never know how you are going to react to a major trauma, but it seems to me that to get us through, hope must remain alive.

When our medical team arrived to help the tsunami recovery, we were unsure about what we would see. We had tried to be prepared for anything—I even asked two counselors to join us in case the situation was too overwhelming for us. Without question, the

situation the Indians faced was too difficult for them. I could not believe the death and destruction and the disturbing stories that were poured out to us all day, every day.

The basic account is this: Fishermen were out in their boats while their wives and children waited on the beaches for the first catch of the day. A big wave came and scared everyone, but it passed and no one suspected what would happen next. The fishermen close to the shore caught sea snakes and fish that belonged in the deep sea. They couldn't understand why such creatures were in their nets. Then it hit—a massive wall of water twenty, thirty, fifty feet high. It came hard and fast, deep into the villages. People tried to outrun it. Mothers grabbing their children made instant decisions of which ones to save. Older children ran hard, some faster than their parents who got caught by the wall of water. People were catapulted into trees and concrete homes. Trees became spears shooting through the water. Most drowned simply because they could not swim.

We stitched up their wounds, sent them for X-rays of broken bones, and gave them cough medicine for the chest colds they caught from breathing in dirty water. We listened and listened to their stories—even with severe wounds and illnesses, they desperately needed someone to hear them. They were afraid. Their beloved sea had turned on them. The ocean they had worshipped for centuries rose up and swallowed them whole and it left the survivors' lives shattered. Guilt ravaged them. Why had they survived and not their family? They wished they had picked up all their children; they wished they had carried an elderly parent; they wished they could have died and someone else had lived. Fear consumed them: How could they trust the elements now? What would happen next? Would the sky reach down and smash them? Would the earth open and swallow them?

Even in the middle of this despair, we sometimes witnessed a smile, a laugh, someone moving forward. Most often it would be a child. Children are as resilient as the creatures of the sea—the sea that almost destroyed them all.

In the midst of the debris and pain, a beautiful boy found a tire and began to play. He played all afternoon, rolling the tire all around the rubble, past demolished houses, bandaged people, and miles of broken boats and tangled nets. He smiled and focused on keeping his tire up and rolling, laughing and trying again when it fell over. He had found hope and it carried him through the destruction that was all around him.

HOSPITALITY

Hospitality is a gift. You must be more interested in relationship with the people coming to your house than in the house they'll see when they arrive. I have learned this lesson over and over. How many times have I thought of inviting someone over but resisted because the house wasn't clean, or I didn't have the right kind of food, or I was simply too busy to extend myself? The Indians seem to have been blessed with the gift of hospitality.

During one of my medical trips in India, our hosts offered to take the team to a new Dalit school in the area. This was a treat because the medical teams often work from sun up to sun down without the chance to experience real life in complex and beautiful India.

At the school, we met a mother bringing her son to class. I asked if we could all go see her home. I thought this would be a valuable opportunity for the team to be inside a Dalit home. The mother quickly jumped at the chance. Imagine dropping your son off at school and returning home with twenty foreigners to entertain!

As we walked to her home she asked if she could make chai for us. I loved the idea but declined the offer because there were so many on the team. I didn't want her to sacrifice precious resources to provide chai for twenty. Chai requires tealeaves, spices, sugar, milk, and water. Many families barely have enough milk and tea for their own daily needs.

Then she told us about her life. She lives with her three children, her aging mother-in-law, and her husband who lost his mind when one of their children was born with cerebral palsy. Her mother-in-law is ill; the daughter with cerebral palsy cannot leave her bed. They share a four-room house with three other families.

Empty water jugs filled their "yard." As the sole breadwinner for her family, she washes clothes for a living, but with the current water shortage, she needs to collect water whenever and from wherever she can. Most of the jugs were empty because she had not found clean water to use lately.

Then it struck me. Hospitality. This woman, this sole provider, eagerly welcomed us into her home and quickly offered her precious water to make us chai - chai for twenty. Without any concern for the water shortage or her need to wash clothes to provide for her family, she extended the hand of friendship to strangers.

If we were truly relational, if we really centered our lives on relationship, perhaps we too could offer hospitality that revolves not around how much water we can offer, but around the intrinsic value of our fellow humans.

SURVIVAL

The medical system in the United States is broken. While we are still able to provide the best medical care to the most people than anywhere else in the world, I don't know anyone working in medicine that wouldn't agree there are major flaws in the system. Too much paperwork, fraud and malpractice, lack of government reimbursement, HMO's and private insurers all create such a complicated system that it begs for reinvention. That's why so many people are working to bring about change to that system. Sometimes it seems an impossibility to overcome such large obstacles.

In India the caste based discrimination the Dalits endure everyday is a huge system that needs to be changed. Our medical team started this day at the local Dalit Education Center—the schoolrooms where those sweet children we sponsor on the internet come to learn and play. Standing outside, the Indian leader with us points to a place in the distance where he has negotiated the purchase of a couple of acres where the permanent school building will be built. It's almost surreal to see actual buildings and land—we work so hard in Denver to put a "face" to the work in India – it's odd to see the real face.

I asked if we could meet the family of one of the schoolchildren and see the inside of their home. We wanted to get a glimpse into the daily life of a Dalit family. The severity of their circumstance almost proved to be too much for some of our team members to witness. The mother we met lives in a four-room house with three other families. She has three children and her mother-in-law living with her. She explained that her husband lost his mind and no longer lived with them. Her oldest daughter has severe cerebral palsy and has spent the last twelve years on a cot in the common living space of this house. Each family gets one bedroom of their own and everyone shares the common area where they prepare food on a propane burner, eat, and clean up. Our hostess washes clothes for a living and she has chosen to send her 6-year old son to the school where she hopes he can learn to make a living that will eventually support the whole family.

My heart broke for the girl with cerebral palsy. I wanted to pick her up, give her a hug and show the mother some exercises that would help her daughter move better. Then I realized she would never have the time. I thought of my friend Karen whose sister's family moved to Europe for an entire year to give their daughter with CP the therapy she needed to help her walk. This girl would never have the opportunity to see a therapist, learn exercises, or have crutches or braces. She will sit on a cot for the rest of her life.

THOSE ARE THE HORRIBLE DETAILS OF THEIR LIFE AND WORDS CAN'T DESCRIBE THE TEARING OF OUR SOULS, THE SCRATCHING OF OUR HEARTS, AS WE TRIED TO INTERACT WITH THIS FAMILY WITHOUT BURSTING INTO TEARS. I DON'T THINK I AM STRONG ENOUGH TO SURVIVE LIFE IN DENVER, MUCH LESS IN INDIA, IF MY HUSBAND HAD BEEN MENTALLY UNSTABLE, MY DAUGHTER HAD SEVERE CP, AND I HAD TO DO MANUAL LABOR TO MAKE JUST ENOUGH MONEY TO EAT A LITTLE.

WHAT CAN I DO FOR THIS WOMAN? WHAT CAN I DO FOR THIS FAMILY? HOW CAN I HELP? A SCHOOL OFFERING QUALITY ENGLISH EDUCATION? A TRANSFORMED COMMUNITY THAT EMPOWERS NEIGHBORS TO HELP ONE ANOTHER? NATIONAL-AID WORKERS CARING ABOUT THIS FAMILY? THAT IS WHAT IS NEEDED. That's what will make a difference in their world. THAT'S WHAT THEY ARE GETTING RIGHT NOW WITH OUR SCHOOL PROGRAM. IT SEEMS LIKE IT IS NOT ENOUGH - AND YET IN MANY WAYS IS EXACTLY WHAT WILL BRING ABOUT REAL LONG-TERM CHANGE.

Empowering the Entitled

There is a big difference between entitlement (having a right to something) and empowerment (enabling someone to do something). The one creates in people the belief that they "should" be rescued, while the other opens their eyes to the fact they have the skills to nurture and rescue themselves. Organizations that work with the poor need constantly to evaluate in which direction their programs are tilting. As a parent, I want my children to eventually live independent productive lives and contribute positively to society. I also want any organization I work with to have the same goal for the poor in the world.

The first time we went to this particular village it looked like a junkyard slum. There was trash everywhere, people were half-naked, their hair was a mess, many had sores all over their bodies, and they were clearly malnourished. The village felt "dark" too—a certain gloominess was everywhere. People pushed and shoved to get to the front of the clinic line. Because they didn't have available medical care or hygiene education, the clinic was extremely busy, treating patients non-stop all day.

One year I returned to this village and saw a striking difference, like night from day. We conducted the clinic in the school building our team had supported. The children were in their uniforms waiting for us. They were all smiling and laughing, their hair combed, skin clean, and bodies nourished. The local volunteers politely said hello and wanted to shake our hands.

The clinic day was calm and peaceful. I certainly treated a lot of patients, but it wasn't a mad house. I had time to walk around and see the village, to play with the children, to quietly think and pray, and to praise God for what He had accomplished here. Clearly, this village was getting good medical care in the weekly clinic. The villagers were much healthier, friendlier, and not as desperate as they had been in the past. Because they had received basic hygiene education, weekly medical clinics, and quality education, their circumstances were improving. It was an overwhelming experience to see how much change could happen in one village.

Then it dawned on me—we've worked ourselves out of a job! Isn't that wonderful? All the prayer, discussions, hard work, and money—it was paying off and making a significant change in the people of this village. They were no longer as needy as they have been in the past.

Entitlement or empowerment: it's in everyone's best interest to empower the people around us.

LEADERSHIP

THERE ARE SO MANY DIFFERING STYLES OF LEADERSHIP. There are currently over 300,000 books on leadership available on line. Each one has it's own take on the proper way to lead. You can become a great leader in 3 steps, 5 easy stages, or 7 progressive ways. You can be a servant leader or an authoritarian leader and apparently both are what people want. Personally, I love growing in leadership skills through conferences, podcasts, books, and advice—but mostly I learn from watching good, and bad, leaders around me.

I learned an important lesson in leadership on one of our medical trips to northern India. We had to take a fifteen-hour non-stop plane ride, a six-hour layover, a two-hour bus ride, and a six-hour train ride to get to our first location. When we arrived late at night there was a crowd of people lined up in the street to see the Americans who had come so far to help them. The next day, as we arrived at the clinic location, I saw a crowd of over 500 people. This was very concerning to me because we typically only started with 50 people and over the day's time would treat around 800. If 500 were already there, would 8000 want to be treated by the end of the day? Our Indian partner explained that they had all come to hear the Americans speak about freedom and to meet the Union Minister (a local politician) who was coming to the opening ceremony of the clinic. The people were more interested in hearing about their emancipation than having their illnesses treated.

The Union Minister was very motivating to the Dalits because she was a woman with a Dalit background—a monumental achievement. She showed dignity and grace throughout the ceremony, even when people walked up onto the stage during the ceremony to give her written petitions requesting money or to explain their problems. I thought she would quickly end this practice—I certainly would have.

THE LONG LINE OF PEOPLE AND THEIR REQUESTS WAS A DISTRACTION TO THE CEREMONY. YET SHE QUIETLY LISTENED TO EACH PERSON. SHE GAVE EACH ONE PLENTY OF TIME TO SPEAK HIS OR HER MIND AND THEN SHE ASSURED EACH PETITIONER SHE WOULD INVESTIGATE THE MATTER AND HANDED THE PETITION TO HER ASSISTANT. What a challenging yet dignity-giving response. THIS UNION MINISTER KNEW SHE REPRESENTED THE PEOPLE STANDING IN THE LINE, NOT THE PEOPLE ON STAGE GIVING SPEECHES.

I DON'T KNOW WHAT KIND OF OVERALL LEADER THIS WOMAN IS, BUT FROM MY PERSPECTIVE, SHE IS A GOOD, COMPASSIONATE, AND A LISTENING LEADER. I'm glad she modeled that leadership style to me.

CONNECTING

I'm often surprised about the way in which I have positively influenced someone. Working in the medical field and social services industries, it's easy to think that the care you give someone is the best way you will make a difference in their life. However, people will often tell me about a small thing I had done that was most meaningful to them. Sometimes these are things that don't seem all that kind, but it still meant a great deal to the other person.

For instance, an old woman walked into our medical clinic with an open wound in her hip. I asked her to lie down so I could see what was wrong. The quarter-sized hole led to a massive infection underneath. It was clear she was in immense pain while I poked around in the wound. We gave her a dozen anesthesia shots, but the infection was so intense we couldn't numb the area, so we cleaned the wound as carefully as we could. I also tried to get a clear history of exactly what happened, but the story wasn't making sense to me. She said she had been beaten with a stick. Then I started pulling out large, hard chunks of something from the wound. That's when I decided to find out exactly what had happened to her, so I asked the interpreter to find out the whole story of her injury.

This woman had committed an unacceptable social crime: as a Dalit, an "untouchable," she had walked on the wrong road. Angry men attacked her for contaminating the road with her presence. Right there on the now "unclean" road, they beat her with a stick breaking her

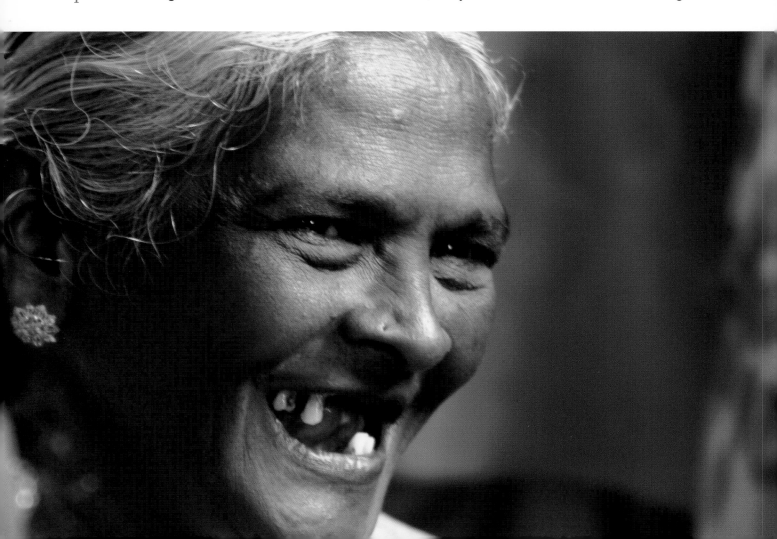

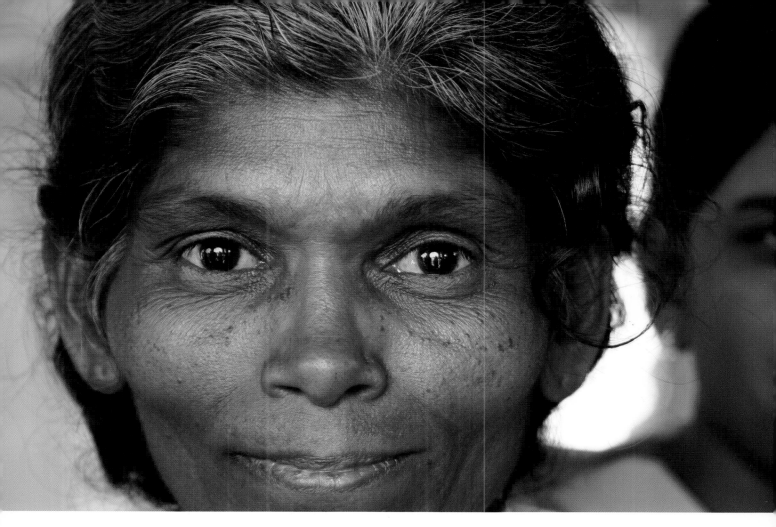

hip and leaving this open wound. The chunks inside her were not pieces of the broken stick, but remnants of her infected bones.

We could do nothing for her. After poking and prodding for thirty painful minutes, we now had to tell her that she needed to go to a hospital for surgery and strong antibiotics. I was on the verge of tears when I explained the situation to her and said that we would gladly pay for her treatment.

I EXPECTED HER TO CRY AS WELL—WE BOTH KNEW THAT HER SITUATION WAS BLEAK. THE REALITY WAS THAT NO ONE IN HER VILLAGE CARED ENOUGH ABOUT HER TO SAVE HER LIFE AND HELP HER GET WELL. Instead, she got down on her hands and knees and kissed my feet. She kissed my feet! I began to sob. Even though no one else cared about HER, SHE WANTED TO THANK ME FOR SITTING WITH HER AND TREATING HER LIKE A HUMAN, EVEN IF IT WAS ONLY FOR THIRTY PAINFUL MINUTES.

OF COURSE I ALWAYS WANT MY PATIENTS TO WALK AWAY HEALED, OR AT LEAST ON THEIR WAY TO BEING HEALED. I WANT TO SEE THAT MY WORK HAS MADE A DIFFERENCE, BUT SOMETIMES--OFTEN TIMES-- it is not the medical intervention that matters, but the power of human connection.

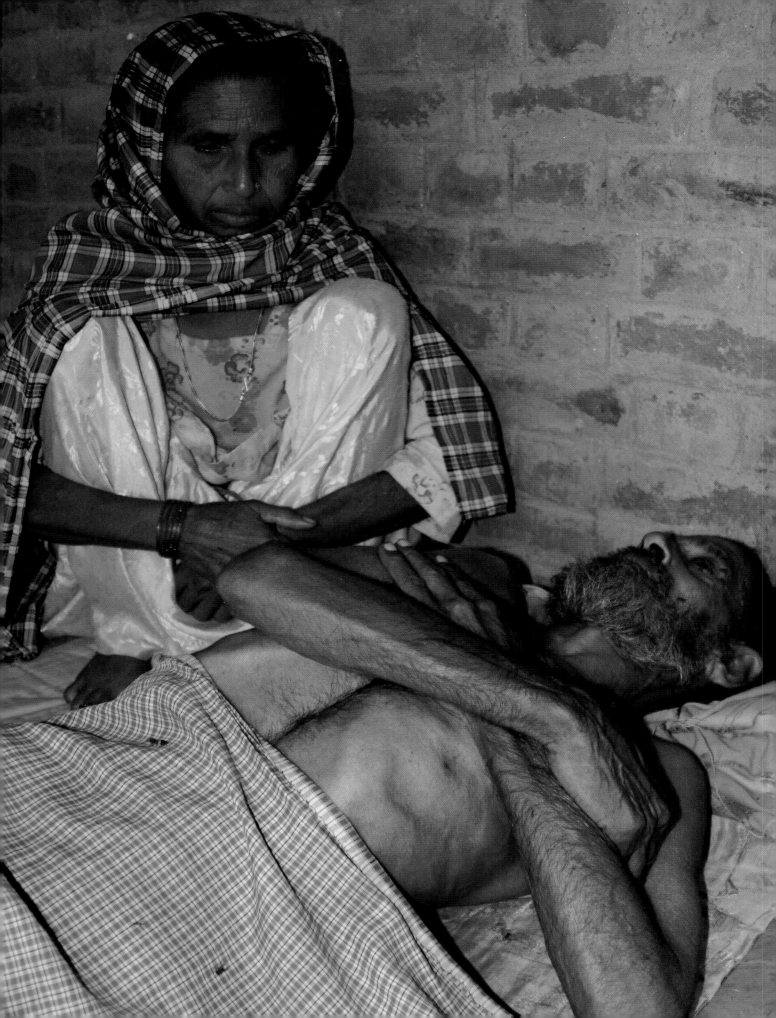

INVISIBLE

I hate being invisible in a crowd, you know, when everyone else seems to know each other and are talking about something you don't relate to. You are present but you might as well not be. I think this is the way millions of Dalits feel about their lives, present but they might as well not be. They are invisible, especially the women. So when I am treating patients in difficult circumstances, I always keep an eye out for the invisible women.

Whenever I am requested to leave the medical clinic to meet someone or see something, I know I am in for a memorable experience. This time, I was invited to meet a man who had been paralyzed for years. It seems that every village has one or two people like this, usually an elderly man or woman who had suffered a stroke, a debilitating fall, or a neurological problem. Their situations are typically dismal—they lie on concrete or hard wooden plinths and are turned from side to side by a supportive family member. Pressure sores inevitably develop leaving the caretaker the daunting task of keeping the wound clean, dry, and free of infection.

We approached a clean concrete home to find an elderly couple on the porch. The woman sat by her husband as he lay on a mat over the hard concrete porch. I smelled the familiar stench of bladder difficulties. With no available catheter or adult diapers and limited water resources, I imagined it was nearly impossible for this woman to keep her husband clean.

The interpreter explained that the man had been paralyzed for fifteen years and that his wife faithfully cleaned his skin every day, turned him every few hours, and massaged and stretched his limbs. Given the circumstances, I was prepared to see large, infected pressure sores. But after inspecting his skin, I could tell someone had been caring very well for him. Aside from a few small sores, his skin looked great.

I turned to the wife and told her how impressed I was with her efforts. I said that it isn't easy to care for someone with as many needs as her husband's and that in all my travels I had never seen anyone who had been cared for as well as him.

SHE SAT UP STRAIGHTER AND A LOVELY SMILE GREW ACROSS HER FACE. BEAMING, SHE TOLD THE INTERPRETER THAT IN FIFTEEN YEARS SHE HAD NEVER HEARD ANYONE APPRECIATE HER EFFORTS, NEVER HAD SHE BEEN VALUED FOR THE SACRIFICIAL CARE SHE PROVIDED IN SUCH A DIFFICULT SITUATION. She had been invisible.

IT DOESN'T TAKE MUCH TO RECOGNIZE THE PEOPLE AROUND US, TO ACKNOWLEDGE THEM SO THEY KNOW THEY ARE NOT INVISIBLE, TO APPRECIATE THEIR CONTRIBUTIONS SO THEY KNOW THEY ARE VALUED.

I Am Somebody

In the last hours of every clinic, a panicked desperation grows in the line of waiting patients. They have lived a calmer desperation their whole lives, but now they are so close to perceived relief—they have walked for hours and waited in line all day with sores on their legs, pain in their knees, frozen shoulders, back aches, neck pain, and fear of the unexplained—that they become restless and anxious. So many people in pain, desperate to have someone give them some hope.

Sometimes I get so focused on getting the job done that I lose sight of the people in front of me. And when the throngs of people come to the medical clinic, I set my sights on treating every patient, so they can each feel like their effort to come to the clinic was worth it. It is a good goal, but often unrealistic.

But, we must stop at dark. We can't see well enough to treat anyone and it is too dangerous to drive late at night. A couple hours before we leave, I switch into "assembly line" mode. Like triaging a battlefield, I work through the line and somehow make judgments about who is "important" enough to treat. How can we pass any of them? It's a wrenching quandary I know all too well: work fast and see everyone, or spend quality time with those who are really hurting and not treat everyone.

The chiropractor next to me, Ali, began to rush in hopes of treating everyone. When a weak and tattered woman approached, Ali doubted she was a good candidate for spinal adjustments and he planned to spend very little time with her. But when he prayed for insight, God told him this woman was a valuable person too——she deserved the best care and all the dignity he could give her—she was somebody. So Ali slowed down, evaluated her, treated the backache, talked to her about her life, and asked if he could pray for her.

As he got ready to bow his head and pray, he asked for her name. In her local dialect she replied: I am "Sumbada"—I am Somebody.

Somebody—she is somebody. Of course she is. Aren't we all? It's obvious, but still I easily get too focused and forget to recognize all the somebodies around me.

Digging Deeper

Through the years I have learned that many times when we talk about our problems, what we say out loud is not the real issue. We talk about being upset about this thing or that, but really we are hurt because of something deeper. Naming that deeper issue can be such a freeing experience, if we have the wisdom and strength to really identify it. Often times we need the help of a close friend or professional to help us peel away the layers of ourselves to reveal what lies at our core.

In India, I had the opportunity to see medically how complex a situation can become when there are too many layers hiding the real issue. Many of the patients who come to the medical clinics in India have never seen a doctor before. They grew up without a scientific understanding of how their bodies work. Because of this, I've had to develop a diagnosis procedure appropriate to their culture. Patients often come to our medical clinics with little ability to describe their ailment and they often link an outside event with their sickness. Often enough that event has nothing at all to do with their disease, but I've learned the art of listening to the history they give, acknowledging that I've heard them correctly, and then probing to figure out what is happening in their body.

One of my favorite physicians, Maurine, is an expert in this technique. She can perceive a patient's disease no matter how convoluted or short the story is that they tell. We needed this skill when a man came into the clinic stiff as a board, walking like Frankenstein. His swollen legs were three times their rightful size and he could barely bend his knees. His shriveled arms looked like symptoms of a neurological disorder and he could not bend his rod-like spine. The scars that covered his abdomen bore witness to hundreds of pain killer injections.

After Ali and I both analyzed his condition and remained perplexed, we called in Maurine. She looked at each area separately and carefully listened to his story. She struggled to decipher all the information before deciding he probably had ankylosing spondylitis—a degenerative disease that gradually renders the spine immovable. The treatments for his neck had probably caused the nerve damage to his arms. He was in so much pain he developed an addiction to narcotics explaining the hundreds of abdominal injections, one of which probably created the systemic infection in his legs.

I showed him exercises for the ankylosing spondylitis and gave him instructions in pressure therapy for his legs. Maurine recommended a further work-up to investigate his kidneys. I think the most important thing any of us did was to pray with him. There were so many layers to his condition, we needed Maurine to help us dig through it all and find the root to his disease.

PEOPLE HAVE LOTS OF LAYERS TO THEIR EMOTIONAL HEALTH TOO. SOMETIMES I THINK I REACT TO BEHAVIOR BASED ON SOMEONE'S INITIAL RESPONSE TO ME. IF THEY ARE COLD AND DETACHED, I STAY ALOOF. IF THEY ARE FRIENDLY AND OPEN, I IMMEDIATELY BEFRIEND THEM. **But people with layers and layers of "baggage" need our friendship the mos**t. THEY ARE REALLY THE MOST INTERESTING ONES AND AFTER SLOWING DOWN TO PROCESS THEIR LIVES WITH THEM, I OFTEN END UP BEING INTIMATELY CLOSE TO THEM.

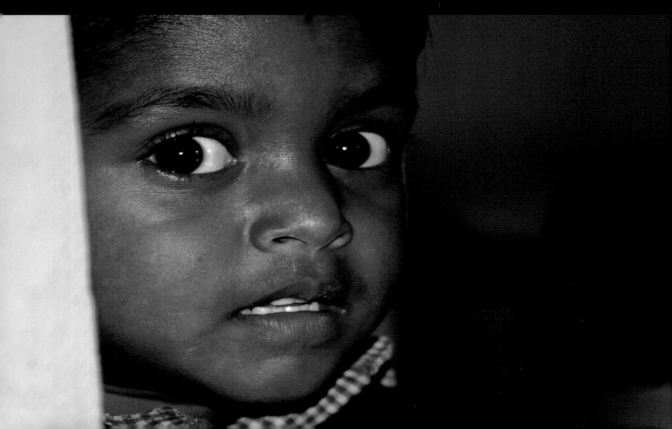

Taking Care of Mom

Traditionally the firstborn Indian son cares for his mother in her old age. When he marries, he and his new wife often move in with his parents to live the rest of their days together. I have heard it said that an Indian woman receives her identity first from her father, then her husband, and finally from her son. If her son loves her and treats her with respect, then she can look forward to her retiring years with him.

When I saw first hand the love and respect of an Indian son for his mother, I was touched by his loyalty. We were the first Americans this northern Indian village had ever seen. The first hours of the medical clinic were slow—people hung back, skeptical of our intentions. Since they were Dalits, they were not used to receiving unconditional help. They watched us, uncertain that we really wanted to give them free medical care without any strings attached. Within hours though, word spread that we were actually helping people, not hurting them, and we weren't asking for anything in return. Patients came from everywhere to receive healthcare for the first time in their lives.

A forty-year-old man came in with a "sore neck." I examined him thoroughly and didn't see anything to warrant his visit. I gave him a massage, some Advil, and showed him exercises and stretches. I assumed he was a "curiosity" patient who wasn't ill but wanted to see the foreigners. Since there was a lull in the patient load, I was able to give him some extra attention even though I was sure he wasn't in any real pain.

An hour later, the same man appeared across the courtyard, very slowly escorting an elderly woman. She crouched over and leaned heavily on a walking stick. When they finally arrived at the clinic, he explained that his mother suffered a stroke six months ago and he wondered if I would help her.

After examination, I showed them strengthening exercises, stretches, and movements to improve her balance. He listened very intently to make sure he understood each exercise perfectly. His obvious love and concern for his mother touched me.

Then it dawned on me that he must have come in earlier as a test to see if I would treat him well. He did not want to subject his mother to a foreigner's care if there was risk that I would be careless or harmful toward her.

If this elderly woman's identity truly was in her son, then his kindness and service freed her to live a life of dignity.

OLD MAN

"Honor your father and your mother, so that you may live long in the land the LORD your God is giving you."

I recently had a conversation about what this verse means exactly. How do you honor an aging father that isn't taking care of himself? How do you treat him with dignity and respect, and still make sure he is safe and well cared for. How do you allow him to be independent and make his own decisions about his future while making sure he is choosing the right path? I guess these are questions we should ask ourselves about many of our relationships. How do we honor those around us in healthy ways?

In American society, when our parents and grandparents get to be a certain age, we act as if they have lived beyond their worth, like they have nothing of value left to give.

The eighty-year-old man who walked into the physical therapy room reminded me why I love the elderly. Their resilience, their spunk, and their wisdom blesses others. They must have something special that sustains them to a ripe old age. In Indian society, especially few live as long as this man—my patient had already outlived the average Indian man by twenty-five years.

IMAGINE THE INDIA OF 1925, WHEN HE WAS BORN. This man from the north Indian state of Punjab has lived through the age of Mahatma Gandhi, Jawaharlal Nehru, and Ambedkar as well as India's independence from British rule and partition. IMAGINE THE WEALTH OF INFORMATION AND EXPERIENCE THAT HE HAS IN HIS HEART AND HEAD.

THIS OLD MAN HAD A BURN ON HIS FOOT THAT WAS OVER A YEAR OLD. THE INFECTION WOULD KILL HIM WITHOUT TREATMENT. AT FIRST, HE DID NOT WANT ME TO CLEAN IT, BUT TOLERATED THE PAIN ANYWAY. I CAREFULLY CLEANED AND DRESSED THE DEEP WOUND. I apologized for making him hurt, rubbed his back, and told him with my eyes and tone of voice that I cared about him. I REALLY WISHED I COULD SPEAK HIS LANGUAGE AND LEARN FROM HIS LIFE EXPERIENCES.

WE DON'T SPEAK THE SAME LANGUAGE—AND YET WE DO. HE GOT DOWN ON HIS KNEES AND TOUCHED MY FEET. I HAD HONORED HIM BY CLEANING HIS WOUND. THIS WAS HIS WAY OF HONORING ME. I wish I could have spent more time with him, hold his hand, drink some chai, and watch the sunset. INSTEAD, I PRAYED THAT WHEN HE WALKED HOME THAT NIGHT SOMEONE WAS WAITING AT HOME TO HONOR HIM.

Help Is In Sight

Life brings so much unavoidable pain and loss that I am frustrated when a tragedy could have been prevented. I guess understanding that great things can still come out of tragedy keeps me going with my work.

When I go on the medical trips to India, I know I will also be presented with situations that are preventable. The areas where the circumstances are the bleakest are also the ones with of the greatest amount of preventable tragedy. I knew we were headed for one such area when we traveled to the quarry pits where people broke rock by hand all day long to support themselves.

Before the clinic ended, our Indian helper Samson wanted me to see a family before they were forced out of their home. This family had three teenage daughters who ran the family store. Having three daughters is a big financial burden to a poor Indian family, because the parents need to pay a dowry for each marriage and there is no son to live with in their retirement.

Last year this family's burden tripled. Each of the daughters had come down with a fever, and when it was done, they were each paralyzed in some way. One could not move her foot, one could not move the left side of her body, and the third could not use her legs. This was devastating for them—they had difficulty working the store, they could no longer walk any distance, and they probably would never marry.

They had contracted Polio. When I stepped outside their small home, I could see on the other side of the quarry pits the hospital that carried the polio vaccination. Since they were Dalits, the community health worker never came into their part of the village to teach them about the importance of vaccinations and to encourage them to take the available shot. Their lives had been changed forever and it easily could have been prevented.

I wish I could stay involved in this family's life to encourage the girls to become educated and to let them know how they are still valued, even though they are paralyzed. I also wish I could see the redemption that is still to come out of their story and to work hard in their community to prevent it from happening to anyone else.

Nowhere to Turn Except . . .

Have you ever been in a situation where you suddenly learn about a horrible tragedy someone has experienced? Someone you have known, but never knew that they had been orphaned, or widowed, or had a terminal illness. They look so normal and put together on the outside, but you instantly see them in a whole new light—strong, courageous, and in need of someone to care for them.

During one of our medical clinics in north India, I left my treatment area to run back to the hotel to retrieve a list of people who needed wheelchairs. When I returned to the clinic, there were all kinds of difficult cases waiting for me. I treated first those I thought I could get through quickly before turning my attention to a paralyzed girl sitting in a wheelchair who had sores on her bottom. Her family had been waiting with her for hours. I was impressed that both her mother and father were waiting in line to make sure she was seen in the clinic. She was just a teenager and had been paralyzed by polio two years before, but I could tell she was well loved.

It was quite a feat to get her onto her stomach in the small examining room, but once I did, I knew we were in trouble because she had weeping wounds all over her bottom. There were five very large wounds—one of them deep enough that I could have stuck my fist in and not reach the bottom. I wanted to cry—I couldn't breathe and wanted to run out of the room. This poor family was living with such a great tragedy and yet they stood in line for hours waiting for me to help them. And what could I really do for her?

If she were in the U.S., we would call in the dietician to talk about protein and proper nutrition, the surgical team to discuss options, and the debriding team to keep her wounds clean and able to heal. Here, however, none of that expertise was available to her. She had no hope—those wounds would kill her if she didn't get help soon. The fact that she was paralyzed made it even worse for me to think about—had she received the available polio vaccination and adequate medical care, she would have been fine.

Her mother had done an excellent job keeping the wounds clean, but the depth of the sores was beyond her ability. I cleaned and dressed the wounds and gave her parents numerous instructions about how to change the dressings, position her on her stomach, shift her weight when she is sitting, and eat protein. I even arranged for her to go to the hospital on our nickel. I told them that she would have to stay there for several months before the wounds healed, if they healed at all. All this advice, while important, seemed too little too late. I had no hope for her.

I asked the parents if I could pray for them. I started to pray and then cry, her Mother and Father were crying, she was crying. I couldn't shake the overwhelming desperation. We needed God to intervene. We couldn't rely on my expertise or that of the people around us, we couldn't rely on good medical treatment or sterile wound care procedures—we only had God and I pleaded the case before Him.

As we cried for the situation, I believe God wept too.

ABRAHAM

There are so many great medical advances and techniques available to us in the United States. I am constantly amazed at what is now possible that never had been imagined when I first went to school. The procedures that are available for burn survivors are incredible. People who have been burned over 90% of their body can recover and live very positive and productive lives. Plastic surgery has made such advances that it seems like anything is possible. But in India, the poor don't have access to good medical care. Dalit people who suffer burns over 30% of their body usually die. The ones who survive do not have access to the wonders of plastic surgery. These truths break my heart whenever I meet someone in India who has survived a burn injury.

Abraham's scar attaches to the skull above his left eye, stretching his eyelid permanently open—he could never close his eye. Sun and constant abrasion have destroyed his cornea. He doesn't have hair on the front part of his head.

I saw this boy's face and immediately fell in love with him. He didn't know when his birthday was, but he knew he was eleven. My own boys, Dillon and Austin, then were ten and twelve. Abraham's demeanor was sweet, but he was clearly aware of his position in society. He understood the implications of living with a severe facial scar. He was also an orphan—his father died when he was a baby, and after he was burned, his mother left him at a hostel. Abraham sees his mother occasionally, but depends on the hostel owners' mercy for food, shelter, and education. Medical care is out of the question for them to provide. It's too expensive and too difficult to worry about for so many children, besides, Abraham's village lacked doctors who could perform the surgery he needed.

The interpreter told me that they could drive Abraham the twenty hours to Cuttack for surgery. Then, in the following months, Abraham would need to travel to Cuttack several more times for follow-up treatment.

I imagined taking him home for surgery and care—he would fit into our family so well. He and Austin would build their own kingdom down by the creek. Dillon would see that we met Abraham's every need. I would love to integrate him into our family, but that wasn't possible. He needed to stay in his motherland because the Indian government didn't allow many adoptions, and certainly not to Americans.

I begged the interpreter to take Abraham to Cuttack for the surgery. I assured him I would raise the money to see that it was done right. This was a huge sacrifice to ask of the worker, but he agreed. He and his wife took good care of Abraham over the next months. They drove him from his home at the hostel to their home in the city to become his surrogate family while he underwent the necessary surgeries.

Later, the worker said, "When my wife told Abraham to sit under the fan he said 'no aunty, I will sit over here because of my eye.' When I took him to the hospital on my bike, his left hand was covering his eye to prevent the wind while the bike was going forward. I felt bad. He suffered a long time—ten years."

WE E-MAILED BACK AND FORTH AS ABRAHAM WENT THROUGH THE RECONSTRUCTIVE SURGERY. AFTERWARD, TEN-YEAR OLD ABRAHAM WROTE A THANK YOU NOTE TO ME: "YOU BROUGHT ME SMILE ON MY FACE NOW I KNOW I HAVE A FUTURE" THE INDIAN TRANSLATOR TOLD ME, "NOW HE CAN GIVE US A BEAUTIFUL SMILE AND IS VERY THANKFUL. I am grateful for this touch of love for this boy this mark is not a mark of burn scars but a mark of love."

I WISH IT WAS NOT TOO LATE FOR HIS EYESIGHT, BUT IT IS. HE HAD NO VISION IN HIS LEFT EYE WHEN I FIRST SAW HIM. ABRAHAM DOESN'T CARE ABOUT THAT THOUGH. HE IS THRILLED THAT HIS EYELID CLOSES AND HIS EYEBALL ISN'T CONSTANTLY HURT BY THE BLOWING WIND AND DUST. HE IS ALSO HAPPY THAT HIS FOREHEAD ISN'T CONSTANTLY STRETCHED AND THAT HE HAS HAIR TO COVER IT.

AND I SETTLED INTO A COMFORTABLE KNOWLEDGE THAT WE DID WHAT WE COULD— WITHOUT THE US MEDICAL ADVANCES—EVEN IF IT ISN'T PERFECT.

ONE DROP

"WE OURSELVES FEEL THAT WHAT WE ARE DOING IS JUST A DROP IN THE OCEAN, BUT THE OCEAN WOULD BE LESS BECAUSE OF THAT MISSING DROP."

MOTHER THERESA

Sometimes all the great problems in the world that need to be addressed overwhelm me. So many people suffer injustices that need international attention, that need our help. But how do we know what to do and for whom to be a voice?

Little did I know three and a half years ago when I first drove into this village that it would become a marker in my life and service to India. This was the first village in India to capture my heart and where I heard the unmistakable call to commit my life to serve the poorest of the poor in the world, the Dalits.

There was so much work to do, so much work already done. The amount of time, money, and emotional energy that goes into getting twenty-eight people and two tons of medical supplies to India for two weeks is unbelievable—the phone calls, the meetings, the e-mails, the discussions, the picking-up and dropping-off supplies day-in and day-out for months. Add in all the other India-centered activities I'm involved in and I find that India has consumed my life. Does it make any difference at all?

On the plane trip over I discussed with God whether serving the Dalit was still what He had called me to do. I'm glad God loves me no matter what because I'm not always the most willing servant. He is so patient with me, even when I whine. I just wasn't sure if all my effort was actually doing anything meaningful because I always seem to be swimming upstream.

Later, exhausted from three hard days of clinics and anxious about the amount of work I knew I already had to do, I hadn't really prepared myself emotionally for driving back into this familiar village. It was fun to recognize the road and see familiar buildings. I actually recognized the first hut in which I treated my first Indian patients, the place where I felt an overwhelming urge to do something more to help the Dalits. I was thinking about that when we rounded the corner and drove up to the school where we would set up clinic for the day. I got out of the car and saw, lined on both sides of the dusty road, girls and boys from the Good Shepherd School dressed in their uniforms and waving at us.

I broke down. It took all I had not to sob uncontrollably in front of them. Here were 150 young boys and girls who two years ago had no chance of getting an education. Some of them had no chance of having a change of clothes and a meal everyday. Now, here they were, all lined up, waving, and saying hello in English. I looked over at my friend and co traveler Kitty who had not seen this village since her journey here three and half years ago. She couldn't believe her eyes. These children had barely survived a cyclone when she was here last. Now they had hope. Now they had a future. You could tell it in the atmosphere. Where there was nothing but desperation, now there was hope.

IT WAS INFECTIOUS AND I TOO REGAINED HOPE. MAYBE ALL OUR EFFORTS ARE MAKING A DIFFERENCE IN THIS LOST AND FORGOTTEN NATION. MAYBE IT IS WORTH ALL THE TIME AND ENERGY.

One drop in the water—you never know how far the ripple might go.

COMMONALITIES

I come from a family of card players, not gamblers, just basic card games. When our friends and families got together, we always ended up playing Hearts, or Spades, or Gin, Gin Rummy, 500, Euchre or even double-bid Euchre. Hearts has been my family's favorite—my dad is incredible at it. I don't know how he does it, but he almost always wins. He has an uncanny ability to count the cards and know what to throw based on what everyone else has already played. We have an ongoing joke about him cheating, usually involving us accusing him of somehow seeing the cards in our hands.

I learned in a place very far away just how universal our family joke to dad was. The island of Khola is out in the middle of nowhere. Even for India, it is out in the middle of nowhere. Some say the island is inhabited with an entire caste of people who migrated together centuries ago to flee persecution. They have lived through monsoons and cyclones that should have wiped them out years ago. There are limited resourced on the island, no running water, no sewage system, no electricity.

I don't know the island's entire story, but I know the first time we arrived most of the inhabitants had never ever seen a white person before. There were dozens of people just standing on the coast, watching us as we passed by in our over-sized canoes. When we landed and unloaded all the medical supplies, people watched our every move as if we were aliens. Children stared as if we were ghosts. Little toddlers screamed and ran to the closest dark-skinned adult they could find.

It was difficult for me to be so set apart from everyone. I knew once I started treating people in the clinic they would warm up to me, but I also wanted to roam the village and connect to people naturally. This was difficult because we seemed so strange and different that they had no interest in letting down their walls. As we walked into the center of the "town" (which was really just an open square of dirt with little "businesses" around the edge) I saw some men playing cards. Often in India men will sit around and play forms of poker and bet money they don't have. I was cautious about the impression I was making with all these people staring at me, but I wanted to see what card game they were playing. I stood close to their foursome for a minute and figured it out right away.

THEY WERE PLAYING HEARTS! THE INTERPRETER THEN TOLD ME THE MAN ON MY LEFT WAS MAKING SURE I WASN'T SOMEHOW SIGNALING TO THE OTHER PLAYERS WHAT HE HAD IN HIS HAND. HA! That could have been my very own father being accused of cheating and wanting to make sure he kept the game clean. I IMAGINED MY FAMILY SITTING RIGHT THERE AND INTERACTING EXACTLY THE SAME WAY, PLAYING THE EXACT SAME GAME. IN AN INSTANT, I WAS JOKING WITH THEM ABOUT WHAT THEY SHOULD PLAY NEXT AND PRETENDING TO KNOW WHAT EVERYONE HAD IN THEIR HANDS AND THEY TORE DOWN THEIR WALLS AND LET ME IN AS ONE OF THEIR OWN.

The game of Hearts.

YOU NEVER KNOW WHAT COMMONALITIES WILL DRAW YOU CLOSE TO PEOPLE FROM THE OTHER SIDE OF THE WORLD.

CHAI

I love chai. Chai simply means "tea," and in India, they boil round tealeaves with milk, sugar, and cardamom to make a fabulous concoction that keeps everyone going throughout the day. The first time I discovered the value of genuine Indian chai, I also discovered its potency. I had hosted an Indian dinner at my house in Colorado and a friend used the authentic ingredients to create a steaming pot of milky, spiced chai. It was so good I sipped and refilled my little cup all evening. When I was still wide-awake at 4:00 am, I realized how effective the caffeine is in chai.

In India, chai is more than a caffeinated drink to sip mid-morning, mid-afternoon, and in the evenings. It is the center of a social practice of sitting and engaging with each other. When you attend a conference in India, it will have as many scheduled break times for tea as times with speakers. This is because Indians are relational, and chai is a way of bringing people together. Villagers who have next to no income prioritize buying the ingredients for their chai, because chai is more than tea to Indians—it is their culture.

The best place to get chai is from some little independent vendor on the back streets of India. In restaurants, I always order "masala chai," but it is never quite as strong or flavorful as the chai you find on the streets. Whenever I go to India, I am on the lookout for "the real thing."

A few people from the team and I walked down the main street in the island village of Khola knowing it would be hours before our heads touched a pillow at the hotel on the mainland. It was our final night in Khola and we had several hours of leisure before the tide rose and allowed us to load the boats and float away. The island was dotted with homes and shops made of mud and rustic wooden planks. The people lived without running water, sewage systems or electricity, unless you counted the generator they brought in that night to show a movie in the town square. As much as we wanted to watch Bollywood's version of Godzilla on the spotty projection, we instead dropped by the local "Starbucks" for a chai.

The shop was really just two thin-planked wooden walls with a thatched roof and a large fire pit in the middle. A husband and wife team ran the shop and I am sure they never expected a crowd of foreigners to step into their business establishment. We started with just four of us and a round of small glasses of "liquid heaven." The owners kept the chai boiling and available, while laughing and talking with each other (probably about how odd it was to have these Americans in their shop).

WE ENJOYED THE CHAI SO MUCH THAT WE INVITED MORE PEOPLE TO JOIN US. BY THE END OF THE NIGHT, WE MADE QUITE A SIGHT WITH TWENTY FOREIGNERS AND INDIANS SQUEEZED INTO THE SMALL STRUCTURE. We rested in the sweet warmth of our tea and began to sing together to our God. WE STAYED SO LONG THEY OFFERED US SECONDS. WE SANG, SIPPED, AND SANG.

ALL OVER INDIA, FAMILIES AND FRIENDS DAILY DRAW TOGETHER AROUND THEIR CHAI. THAT NIGHT WE TOO SHARED A BEAUTIFUL TIME OF UNITY WITHIN THE TEAM AND WE TOO CAME TO UNDERSTAND AND APPRECIATE THE VALUE OF THIS CULTURAL INDIAN CHAI EXPERIENCE.

Numbered Days

Do no harm. This is the first rule of conduct for all international medical organizations. Medicine has a lot of nuances to it, and when you practice cross-culturally, there is a lot of room for misinterpretation that comes into play. Medical practitioners must therefore always keep a humble heart and work hard to correctly interpret the conditions of their patients.

After an eventful 2-hour boat ride on the Bay of Bengal, we arrived at Khola, a special island to anticipate visiting and to remember the rest of the year. Khola is a simple farming community, like all the other villages in India, yet there is a beauty here that we don't find elsewhere. The beauty isn't in the picturesque landscape of green rice fields and grazing cows. It isn't the handsome mud huts painted with white designs. It isn't even the unusual scene of fences around all the houses.

The island's beauty comes from the attitude of the people. They are so kind and friendly, not only to us but to each other. We don't hear the yelling and shouting that serves as the backdrop in so many villages. We don't see all the pushing and shoving while people wait to see a doctor. And the people are clean despite the lack of running water and electricity.

I cannot imagine what these poor people did during the cyclone of 1999—where did they find shelter on their little island? How did they cope? The government has since built a cyclone shelter—it is a mass of concrete. I cannot imagine how they got all the equipment and supplies here to build it. It is probably twenty feet in the air resting on huge concrete pylons with a half dozen 20x20 rooms at the top. I'm not sure it would hold all the residents of Khola, but at least it is better protection than the huts they had during the last cyclone. We used some of the rooms in the cyclone shelter to conduct our clinic.

The story of what happened isn't clear but the first thing to happen the morning of our first day was an elderly man (his family says he's 95) was walking up the concrete steps of the shelter when he slipped and fell. One of our team members rescued his head from hitting the concrete, but unfortunately, the impact on the rest of his body was strong enough to fracture his hip.

They rushed him over to my room. It was chaotic with villagers screaming and crowding in, and two different doctors trying to take histories and shout orders. I took the old man's blood pressure and it was extremely high, but mine was too with all the commotion. We decided he was stable and took him outside to rest. Later I went out to decide what we could do for him.

A fractured hip in a 95-year old man is a grave injury. Even in the U.S., I'm not sure there are many places that would operate on him. Bed rest and traction to reduce the fracture were the best we could offer him. If we took him anywhere, it would be a half hour cart ride to the dock, a two-hour boat ride to the mainland, and then a four-hour car ride to the nearest hospital. He chose to stay on the island.

Seamus, an EMT who also proved to be a great ortho-tech too, devised a traction system we could set up for him in his daughter's hut. It took quite some time to construct the system, get the man stabilized enough to travel back to his daughter's (on a cart powered by a bicycle), and then get ourselves there too.

We set him up in traction, loosened the unit to make sure the blood supply wasn't being cut off, explained the treatment to the family, and sat for a while and prayed with him. What else could we do? I felt so helpless. I held his hand. I smiled at him. I massaged his sore muscles. How could I reach out to him and show him the love I know. I "talked" to him (me in English he in Bengali). We prayed again and then Seamus and I went back to the clinic.

I expected the old man to die soon from this accident, but we would not be on Khola long enough to know. The statistics for an injury like this are not good. I'm not sure of exact numbers, but in the U.S., something like 90% of everybody over 90 who breaks a hip dies from it. Surely this man's days were numbered.

I thought about him often when I got back home. I knew it would be a whole year before I could find out about him, so I prayed. The next year the tsunami hit. Our annual medical trip to the island of Khola was changed so we could visit the villages farther south that had been affected. This was another year of wondering, so I kept praying. The next year our team did not return to Khola, but instead went to other needy areas. Another year of wondering, and I kept praying.

Finally, three years later, our team returned to Khola. I tried to find someone who knew the man to find out what had happened to him. I was overjoyed to hear that he had lived! He survived his fracture—it took him months to recover, but he did and he was walking around six months after the accident. Unfortunately he had died a few months before our team came back, but not from complications of a hip fracture.

So what does it mean to do no harm in this situation? This man could have fractured his hip in a number of different ways. Some medical professionals believe the elderly actually fracture their hip first, and then they fall. No matter how his fracture happened, I do know that we did the right thing for him- and that goes beyond "Do no harm."

FOOD FIGHT

I used to go to medical conferences that I would describe as "work hard— play hard." To defend a research paper before this crowd was like standing before the Spanish inquisition; but at night, boy, those expert professionals certainly could let their hair down. I think those experiences in the evening helped this group of people band closer together for their difficult work during the day. They were the best of the best in their professions and a close-knit family spread all over the country. They say that "crisis" brings people close, but sometimes I think it is just plain "fun" that knits us together. I fully embrace that attitude on medical trips.

On one trip, forty medical team members descended upon the small fishing dock nestled between a mud hill and the sea. Scattered among the oversized canoes, fishermen sold reeking mounds of fish. They had come to know us there, and greeted us eagerly. Doctors, dentists, physician assistants, nurse practitioners, physical and occupational therapists, nurses, pharmacists, Americans and Indians—we all crammed into two shaky canoes and pushed into the open waters of the Bay of Bengal.

The Americans took this in-stride—we all learned how to swim when we were children. I felt horrible for the Indians because most of them could not swim at all. One Indian doctor talked non-stop during the two-hour boat ride out of sheer nervousness that the boat would sink and he would drown. To lighten the tense atmosphere, we started competing with the other canoe to see who could go faster. Each twenty-foot canoe had a two-cylinder engine attached to it so we could chug along in the water.

In the middle of the brackish ocean canal, our engine stopped. We were "dead in the water." In the uneasy silence, we called to the other boat for help. Laughing because they clearly had "won" the contest, they tied a towline from their stern to our bow. A new tense silence overtook us as we all pondered how two canoes, forty professionals, and dozens of boxes of medical supplies could make it through the Bay waters on one tiny engine.

I heard a splash and turned to see a tomato in flight toward our boat. Before we knew it, both boats were engaged in an all-out food fight. Built-up tension and stress gave way to robust laughter and rambunctious shouts. Leftover breakfast soared in the space between us. We constructed a giant slingshot to torpedo latex-glove water-bombs. They filled entire water bottles and threw them at us. Indian nurses orchestrated an assembly line to build torpedo ammunition. Everyone had great fun.

THIS WHOLE PHENOMENON FASCINATES ME: MATURE PROFESSIONALS WHO SACRIFICED TIME AND MONEY TO COME SERVE THE PEOPLE OF INDIA AND INDIAN PROFESSIONALS WHO HAD DEEP RESPECT FOR THEIR PROFESSION AND THEIR REPUTATIONS, all acting like five-year olds—hurling objects through the air, ducking ammunition so their neighbor takes the hit, laughing at the harmless demise of others. IS THIS OUR REACTION TO THE STRESS OF POSSIBLY DYING IN THE MURKY WATER OF THE BAY OF BENGAL? WERE WE RELEASING BUILT-UP TENSION FROM THE INTENSE MEDICAL CLINICS AND GRINDING POVERTY? ARE WE ALL JUST LITTLE FIVE-YEAR OLDS INSIDE? YES......MAYBE ......PROBABLY......AND IT FEELS GREAT.

Joy, suffering, fear—all entangled in two boats, forty people, and leftover food.

CRUSHED EXPECTATIONS

The more I travel to India, the more I realize how similar people are everywhere in the world. Almost everyone wants simple answers that are quick and painless. Sometimes our medical team gets discouraged because most of the villagers just want a prescription for pills that will take their pain away without having to do anything else. I can't really blame them. They live in such difficult circumstances with little understanding of how their bodies work, but we are the same way in the United States. If there was a pill to help our muscles get stronger without exercise, you had better believe people would line up for miles to get it.

Last year I was working in my room with a couple of patients when a mob of people came crashing through the door, four of whom were carrying a man like a bag each holding an extremity. His wild screams made me think he was being pulled apart by his "rescue squad."

He was a captain who slipped off his boat into the canal and was smashed between two vessels before sinking into the water. He had been terrified of water because he couldn't swim. His friends knew our medical team was "in town" because we had been at the boat dock the day before on our way to Khola Island. They "four-man carried" him for over a mile to our clinic. After a thorough examination and plenty of screaming from the patient, we decided he had broken his wrist, twisted his knee, and bruised his jaw.

I made him a splint for his wrist, gave him an ice pack for his jaw, and splinted his knee. He was quite beat up and I didn't have much hope that he would heal well enough to get fully back to work. He had been so hysterical that he spent a long time in my examination room trying to settle down and ready himself for the trek back to his house. I gave him instructions about how to keep everything stable for the next few months, but doubted he would follow them. I also worried that the near-drowning experience put him at great risk for a deadly lung infection.

When I returned a full year later, the captain paid me a visit again. His smooth gait and speech showed a well-healed knee and jaw. His wrist had good motion too, and though his knee was sore, the ligaments were intact. I was pleased to see how well he had healed.

I greeted him and found that he was frustrated. He complained about his knee hurting and that he couldn't walk as well as before the accident. A ligament test verified his knee had healed well, but since he had babied his injured knee, his muscles were far too weak, so I did the only thing that would help him: I showed him simple exercises to build-up the muscles that strengthen and protect his knee.

Unfortunately, he wasn't interested in exercises.

I spent twenty precious minutes with him as others waited in line, trying to talk him into doing the exercises for ten minutes each morning and night. But still he wanted—expected—me to give him a magic pill to fix his knee.

Don't we all want that pill? We think we know what we need and get frustrated when it isn't handed to us on a platter. Often our problem is simply a shift in perspective—we take a situation for which we should be grateful and turn it into cause for a festering sense of victimization. I thought that this man, living in rural India, crushed between two boats, with no access to other medical care, had fared rather well. Sadly he thought his knee should work as well as it had before.

What a difference in perspective.

Isn't this what we believe of God? We say, "Just give me what I want and everything will be great," but God wants us to train hard. He does not give us all the answers, all the easy pills. He wants to make us stronger, but often we are too weak to do our exercises.

Safety Behind the Walls

I used to think communes were the answer to life. Growing up a Quaker, they were part of our extended community. I thought they held the golden key: life in wonderful harmony with good people, walled off from the terrible wicked world around us. It still sounds a little appealing.

But that's not the world to which I am called. I cannot truly live my faith if I do not live in global community with those in need. I decided in college that responsible Christians must spread love and hope to the world around them, especially to the dark places.

These convictions led to strong, albeit uninformed opinions about mission compounds as well. I know they are different from communes, but I don't think I could justifiably hide behind mission walls, just as I couldn't hide in a commune.

With that mindset, I spent three glorious days and nights behind the walls of a mission compound in India. When a man named Paul built the community decades ago, the donated property sat in a desert. He built a large pipeline to bring water to the area. He built a wall around the entire property to protect the inhabitants. He built a chapel, a guesthouse, living quarters, a primary school, a secondary school, a college, seminary, roads, and walking paths. He planted gardens, woods, and grass.

Today over 1,800 orphans, 700 seminary students, and enough staff to run the compound live there—over 2,500 people in all living their faith in varying degrees of complexity. The orphans who would have been living on the streets, or worse, now attend school, eat three times a day and sleep indoors away from the evil that lurks outside at night. And the students now have the opportunity to learn about the God who calls them to serve others.

From the moment of our arrival, our hosts welcomed us warmly and showed us splendid hospitality. After a long week of nonstop work, it was a welcomed respite for our tired bones. We slept in bunk beds, washed with bucket showers, and left refreshed to conduct medical clinics each day. When we returned at the end of the day, my heart felt it could rest and agree to be at peace for a while. God's strength is present here in a way that doesn't exist outside these walls. We spent two hours each evening in chapel with the seminary students from all over India worshipping with such synergy and strength that I am sure they heard us in the city 30 kilometers away. Inclusiveness, acceptance, fellowship, and God's presence permeates everything.

I guess I've changed my opinion about mission compound walls. There

ARE GOOD REASONS FOR THESE PLACES OF SECURITY. I'VE CHOSEN, HOWEVER, NOT TO LET THE REFUGE OUTWEIGH MY GOD-GIVEN CALL TO SERVE THE WORLD OUTSIDE.

IN SOME WAYS WE ALL HAVE COMPOUND WALLS IN OUR LIVES. IT MIGHT BE OUR SUBURBAN HOMES WITH HIGH FENCES AND STRONG DOORS. MAYBE IT'S JUST A ROOM IN OUR HOUSE WHERE WE GO TO "GET AWAY FROM IT ALL." SOME OF US HAVE WALLED OFF OUR HEARTS FROM AN INTIMACY THAT COULD BE OURS. My dream is for those walls built around our hearts not to keep us safe at the expense of God's calling. GOD WANTS TO CREATE SAFE PLACES IN OUR WORLD WHERE WE CAN REST IN HIM, BUT HE ALSO WANTS US TO LEAVE THE COMPOUND WALLS AND REFLECT HIS GLORY TO THE WORLD.

Soul Touching

Often times it's not until the moment is gone that we realize how important it actually was. This was the first day of my church's fourth annual medical trip to India. I treated a woman who someone found walking around the village. She clearly had leprosy and her right foot was in bad shape. All five toes were black and her skin was as hard as leather. The sole of her foot had one large open sore with repugnant infected pus all around.

I felt bad about my treatment—I worked the best I could but the circumstances were all wrong. I probably spent half an hour with the sole of her foot, but I really wanted to spend more time connecting with her soul. It was the end of the day and my team members stood in my room talking because they were finished with their own patients. I cut through each toe to expose the tissue. I scrubbed and cleaned everything I saw. Then I wrapped it all up with these great wound care materials that eat away at the infection and encourage healthy skin growth.

But I didn't feel good about the whole situation. There were so many people in the room, so much commotion, lots of focus on her foot. That was the problem. All the focus was on her foot.

I wanted to change the ambience for this wonderful lady with leprosy if only for a moment. Sure, I cleaned up her foot, but did I touch her soul? That's what I wanted to do. That is what I am here for. I want to be about touching souls not just soles. I think we do touch souls. Every time I look into someone's eyes, I connect with their soul and I want to reach out and let them know there is a better life waiting for them. I want to cradle them and protect them from all the pain of their world. I want to let them know there is love and grace and mercy just waiting to fill their lives.

I didn't get a chance to meet this lady's soul. I didn't get a chance to reach out to her. I didn't get a chance to make time stand still for just one moment and let her know that she was loved. I just cleaned up her foot.

She came back the last day of clinic and her foot was much better. Her toes weren't black, the wound on her sole was clean, and it looked like she may heal—this time. I cleaned everything up again and dressed it with the best wound care products the world has to offer. With good care, she might keep her foot. I rubbed her back and talked to her and looked into her eyes...

...but I fear the moment for soul touching was lost that first day.

STENCH

I had heard so much about the people in the quarry pits before I finally had a chance to visit them. On a medical trip to south India, we traveled a short distance outside a major city to bring medical care to the people in the quarry pit.

These people are modern day slaves. Early each morning they slip from their homes that sit on the edge of quarry cliffs and slide down the rock to the bottom. With primitive tools and great strength of will they break rocks all day long for a little income. Unfortunately, the whole family is involved in this work—some children as young as three or four break rocks for ten hours each day. Children who would be attending preschool in the United States are instead sliding down 50-foot rock cliffs each morning to break rocks so they can have enough rice to eat that night.

A loan shark runs the operation. The workers are those who owe him money. These people owe so much they will never be free. Their meager income barely pays the interest. Most of them borrowed from the loan shark as a last resort to provide urgent medical care for a family member. If they wanted hope of saving their loved one, the only option was to borrow the money and pay the hospital bill up front.

Flies swarmed everywhere. Clouds of pestering insects swarmed the air, like the insect repellent commercial where a man sprays himself and enters a tent full of mosquitoes to prove the repellent's effectiveness. But this time they are flies, not mosquitoes, and we cannot escape the tent.

I worked all day cleaning wounds and keeping them free from the flies' sabotage. People, like this little girl, stood in line to be treated while they covered their faces from the smell. When I took a break and walked behind the clinic, I faced mountains of garbage piled high and rolling down the quarry walls. The stench was suffocating. This was the source of the smell and flies.

THE POWERS THAT BE HAD RECENTLY DECIDED THEY WERE DONE WITH THIS QUARRY AND THEY DID NOT NEED THE PEOPLE'S SERVICES ANYMORE. THE PLAN TO DISPERSE THE COMMUNITY WAS TO SEND GARBAGE TRUCKS TO THE QUARRY TO DUMP MOUNTAINS OF INFESTED GARBAGE UNTIL THE VILLAGE COULD NO LONGER ENDURE THEIR OWN HOMES. THEY WERE TRYING TO FORCE THE PEOPLE TO MOVE. THIS COMMUNITY HAD NOWHERE ELSE TO LIVE, HOWEVER, AND NO WAY TO ESCAPE THE LOAN SHARKS WHO THREATENED THEIR VERY EXISTENCE.

These modern day slaves were not even welcome in their own prison.

GOOD-BYE

I value a proper good-bye. If someone has meant something to me, then I invest the time to let them know I appreciate them. I never know whom I will or will not ever see again in life, and every time I leave someone, I want to make sure they know I care for them. I don't always do such a good job with this, but I wish I did. This point was driven home to me as I came to know and love a beautiful Indian woman.

When I finally looked up from my work, I could hardly believe what surrounded me: two surgeries to remove cysts, an infant cradled in her mother's arms waiting for me to pack her wounds, a young man waiting for us to cast his broken foot, Seamus tending to the man with the fractured hip, Caroline explaining exercises to a young woman, and Sara (my Indian interpreter) darting from one place to the next interpreting this foreign local dialect for each of us. Every time I thought I was getting overwhelmed at trying to be everywhere at the same time I would think of Sara who filtered all the information for us to hear.

Sara and I worked together from morning till night. We had seen simple knee and back pain, diabetic ulcers, paralysis of all types, leprosy and polio patients, and children with untreated special needs.

She was a gem. With a great medical aptitude, she quickly became more than an interpreter. She learned the process of evaluating physical therapy patients so that by the end of the second day she could accurately predict what treatment I might prescribe. I could easily trust her to explain exercises to patients while I moved on to the next in line. I always bond with the interpreter, but this year I formed a deep respect for this young woman who persevered with a smile on her face.

On the last day at 3:50 she unexpectedly whispered in my ear that she would be leaving in ten minutes. With a whole crowd still waiting to be seen, I thought of how we still had so many to serve. Then I realized I wouldn't get to say a proper goodbye, to send her off well and let her know she matters.

Sara suddenly threw her arms around my neck and started crying, "Pray for me, Aunty. Pray for me and my mother. My brother is in a fundamentalist political party that oppresses people of other faiths, and he doesn't like us being Christians. He beats us and we are not safe. I must go back to Kolkutta where we live. Pray for me, Aunty." She hugged me again and ran to catch her ride.

WHY DID SHE WAIT UNTIL THE LAST MINUTE TO TELL ME THIS NEWS? HOW COULD I HAVE WORKED SO CLOSELY WITH HER, DEPENDED ON HER, APPRECIATED HER SO IMMENSELY AND NEVER REALLY KNEW WHAT HER LIFE WAS LIKE?

I KNEW HER AS A GIFTED MEDICAL INTERPRETER IN THIS CLINIC, YET HER LIFE ENCOMPASSED SO MUCH MORE. I wish I had known everything about her. I wish I had the opportunity to give her a proper good-bye.

STARVING

I love children. Big ones, small ones, dirty ones, and misbehaving ones—they all capture my heart. When children with special needs come through the line at the medical clinic, I want to spend extra time with them. I like to assess their strength and see if I can teach their families some exercises. I want to encourage their parents, explaining the ways to carry, speak to, feed, clothe, and plan for the future of their child. As a mother who was also once in their frightening position, I want to share with them the realistic hope for the future and the understanding that their child is a true gift from God.

When I heard about a very sick child in the registration line, I wanted to see her right away. Some thought she had cerebral palsy and I wanted to investigate it just to make sure, but that wasn't the problem.

She was a three and a half year old girl who looked like a 9-month old baby. Her muscle tone was normal and she had accuracy in her movements, but her limbs were toothpicks with joints like a patient with Ricketts. She had an echo in her cry, but wasn't noticeably mentally disabled.

Starving. This girl was starving—that was her struggle.

The poor girl had been slowly starving to death. The doctors confirmed it. She suffered severe malnourishment and needed immediate hospitalization. We made the arrangements to get her life-saving treatment. Her widowed mother had not been able to care for her adequately. Her husband had died three years ago leaving her and her child to figure out how to make a living on their own in a society that looks down on widows. This poor mother had done the best she could to scavenge food from here and there, but it was not enough to meet the needs of her growing and developing baby daughter.

Starving for three and a half years! How many meals did I enjoy in those years while this baby slowly starved? How many times have I thrown out spoiled food in my refrigerator or left food on my plate? How often have I tried to diet because I OVER-eat? Everyday there are 41,000 children who die of starvation somewhere in the world. Everyday.

I CANNOT CHANGE THE WHOLE WORLD—SO MANY PEOPLE FACE BITTER NEED. BUT I CAN SEEK OUT AND HELP THIS ONE LITTLE GIRL. I MUST. WHEN THE APOSTLE JAMES WROTE THAT TRUE FAITH IS TO CARE FOR THE WIDOWS AND ORPHANS, GOD KNEW HE WOULD CREATE THIS PRECIOUS LITTLE GIRL. MAY WE HAVE MORE TRUE FAITH AND MAY WE JOIN GOD IN SHOWING THOSE PEOPLE OUR SOCIETY HAS DISCARDED THAT GOD DOES NOT FORGET THEM.

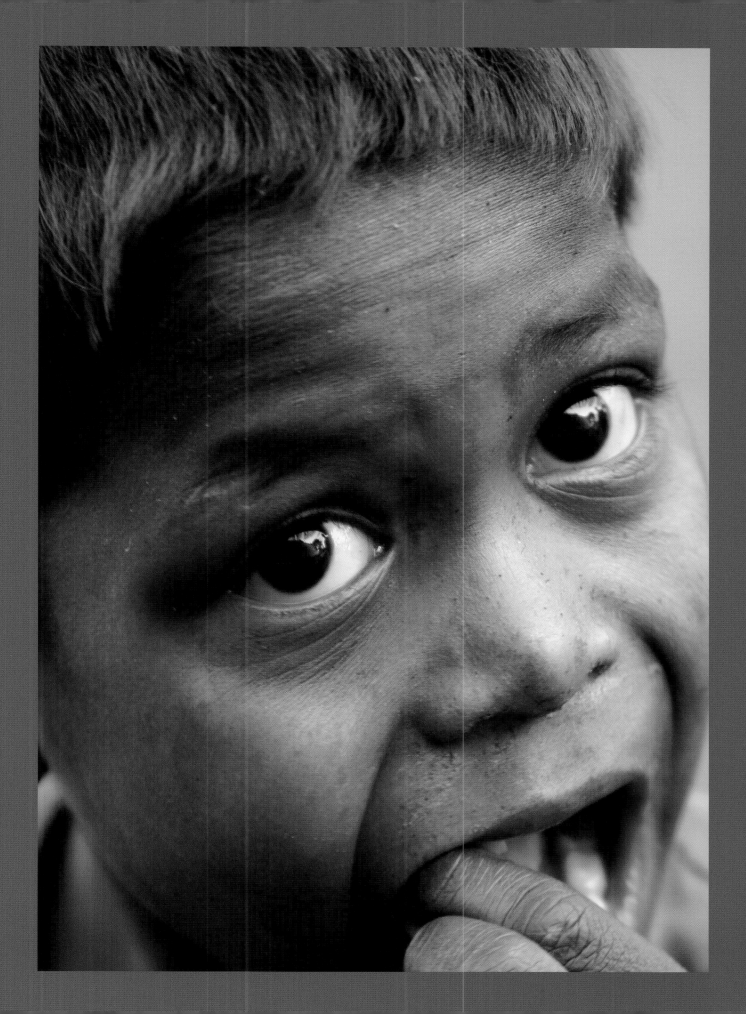

BEAUTY

I heard a talk once about how God created us with an internal sense of beauty. The speaker described how decorating our homes helped connect us to that internal sense. I wasn't too sure about what she said. I don't know, it just seemed a bit trite. Was she just rationalizing the amount of time she spent decorating her own home?

When I traveled 20,000 miles to the opposite side of the world for the first time, I found myself in a remote Indian village among the Dalit, some of the poorest people in the world. Most of them struggle to live in 10x15 foot huts with meager roofs and failing mud walls. Their main sustenance comes from simple rice and lentils (dhal). Those who own more than a few sets of clothes feel blessed. Some rural Dalits are fortunate enough to own livestock that, naturally, live in their huts with them. One could easily get depressed looking at the dirty and oppressed circumstances of their lives.

What impressed me the very first time I walked in a village, though, was the unbelievable inclination for color, beauty, and symmetry. Women who owned only one or two changes of clothes wear radiant saris. Mothers with too many children to feed, who work all day long to provide for them, paint intricate designs with rice water on the outside walls of their mud homes. Fruit vendors who barely earn a living stack their fruit in such detailed displays that I hesitate to buy any for fear of disturbing the works of art.

IN A LIFE DOMINATED BY DIFFICULTIES, INESCAPABLE DUST, AND A LACK OF BASIC RESOURCES THESE VILLAGERS STILL FIND WAYS TO EXPRESS THEIR TRIUMPHANT URGE TO CREATE AND SURROUND THEMSELVES WITH BEAUTY.

As creatures in the image of a creative God, PERHAPS THIS IS THEIR WAY TO LIVE THAT TRUTH.

VESSELS OF MUD

In 1983, I lived in a town that had an official "government green sign" that said, "No blacks allowed out after dark." Reportedly, this law was to protect darker-skinned people from harassment. Right. It is difficult to believe such blatant racial discrimination still exists in America. We all have mental images of signs posted over drinking fountains and at restaurants, "No colored allowed" or "Colored only." I can't imagine what it would do to my self-image to be constantly reminded that I was separated from the rest of society, devalued. It is one thing to believe that on your own and quite another to see signs all over town reminding you that everyone else thinks you are worthless. Although we no longer have official government signs in the United States that remind others of their separateness, I wonder what cues we give people to tell them that they are below us.

In India, there is a "two vessel" system. This means that if you are Dalit you must eat and drink from vessels that would not touch the mouths of higher caste people. Many people have separate glasses in their homes to offer drinks to their domestic servants. These glasses even look different from the regular household dishes.

I have a well-respected Dalit friend who travels all over the world to speak at international conferences on behalf of the Dalit movement. In his home village, he has friends who are from a higher caste. When he goes back for a visit he is often invited into their homes for a cup of tea, but he is offered the tea in a separate vessel from the others. He drinks from the "Dalit cups" in the home of his friends. Sitting around a table chatting about life he holds in his hands the reminder that he is not equal to his colleagues.

HISTORICALLY, CLAY CUPS WERE USED BY RESTAURANTS, TEASHOPS, AND TRAIN STATIONS IN INDIA TO SERVE THE DALITS. WHILE OTHER PATRONS WOULD DRINK FROM CHINA, THE DALITS WOULD DRINK FROM THESE VESSELS MADE FROM MUD. WHEN THEY WERE DONE DRINKING, the Dalits would throw the cup on the ground to break it into pieces, ENSURING THAT NO UPPER CASTE PERSON WOULD BE CONTAMINATED BY DRINKING AFTER A DALIT. TODAY CLAY CUPS ARE COMMONLY USED ALL OVER INDIA AND ARE NO LONGER EXCLUSIVE TO THE DALIT POPULATION. YOU WILL FIND PILES OF USED BROKEN CUPS BY OUTDOOR TEASHOPS. EVEN TODAY, THOUGH, THE DALITS ARE SERVED FROM SEPARATE VESSELS AS A CONSTANT REMINDER THAT THEY ARE UNCLEAN.

AS THEY WALK THROUGH THEIR DAY, THEY SEE THE PERPETUAL REMINDER THAT THEY ARE CONSIDERED TO BE LESS THAN, NOT WORTHY, SEPARATED.

DOWN BY THE RIVER

I don't like the old adage "Don't talk about religion or politics with your friends." I don't understand that perception. We should always create an environment safe enough to stand for our own beliefs and still actively listen to the beliefs of people with opposing viewpoints. In the United States, we have the privilege of choosing what spiritual belief we desire to pursue. Parents hope their children grow and choose their parents' faith, but it is generally understood that each person should choose for him or herself.

Indian culture has been predominantly Hindu for 3,000 years. Varied as those years of culture appear, "Hinduism" literally means "the religion of India." People in minority religions face many struggles—for many, especially those in the low castes, leaving Hinduism can mean total rejection from family, losing a job, facing discrimination, violence, and even death.

Yet there I sat on the side of a riverbank, watching people arrive by foot, in trucks, and on open-air livestock beds. They didn't care how they got to the river, they just wanted to get there. Nearly 1,000 people wanted to choose their faith publicly, to be baptized as Christians. Over the course of the morning, these people came down the riverbank and into the frigid water to become a follower of Christ.

Words cannot describe what it was like to watch this joyous occasion. I was surprised by the unhindered celebration—it wasn't at all like the reflective baptisms I've witnessed in the US. The Indian pastors stood in the river for hours, singing songs while everyone clapped. Since most have never taken swimming lessons, they rarely immerse themselves in water. So they went under the water afraid, but came back up smiling, joyful, and splashing with delight.

IT WAS STRAIGHT OUT OF THE NEW TESTAMENT—YOUNG PEOPLE WERE BAPTIZED TOGETHER AND OLD PEOPLE CAME OUT OF THE WATER WITH CANES AND HELPING HANDS. THE DRIVER OF AN OX-CART STOPPED ON THE BANK ABOVE TO WATCH THE SPECTACLE. WATER BUFFALOS SWAM BY TO GET A CLOSER LOOK AS ONE BY ONE PEOPLE TOOK A STEP OF FAITH, OPENLY DECLARING THEY WERE CHRISTIANS IN A COUNTRY THAT DOESN'T LIKE PEOPLE TO CONVERT TO OTHER RELIGIONS. They weren't thinking about the persecution they would soon suffer, THEY WERE FOCUSED ON CELEBRATING THEIR NEWFOUND SPIRITUAL JOURNEY. THEY WERE THINKING ABOUT BEING A CHILD OF THE GOD OF THE UNIVERSE.

AND I GOT TO SIT ON THE RIVERBANK AND WATCH.

SANCTUARY OF PEACE

It is said that for everything that is true about India, the opposite is also true. India is a country of immense dirt and intense beauty; it has the greatest number of millionaires and the largest population living below the poverty line, crowds of people, and sanctuaries of peace.

The city of Kolkutta is a perfect example of this. Kolkutta, (formally known as Calcutta) was made famous by Mother Theresa. She founded several facilities in this city, but one of the most well known is her Home for the Dying Destitute. In the square mile surrounding this place you will find the most unusual collection of people. Some from the beggar caste have been surgically deformed so they can beg for money on the streets, their deformities defying what you might normally see. The poorest of the poor lie on blankets on the side of the street waiting to be rescued. Vendors sell their wares as they understand this location has become a tourist spot for foreigners from around the world. Mothers cook over open fires while their half-naked children run in and out of the street begging for money. Cattle are everywhere often blocking traffic.

Behind Mother's Home of the Dying Destitute lies the Hindu Kali temple of destruction and death. They still perform animal sacrifices at this temple and it is not uncommon to witness a sacrifice and watch people drink the animal's blood as it pours onto the floor. The stench of the blood, the rotting animal, the excrement from cattle and humans, and the smoke from the fires linger in the air. It is completely overwhelming, even for India. It's difficult to compose yourself and try to put all the images together in your head and heart.

As I entered the Home for the Dying Destitute, the smell, noise, and disarray of the world outside dissipated and all I could focus on were the dozens of patients lying on beds waiting to die. It was if time stood still and the emotional confusion of the world outside shrunk down to the clarity of life and death. Here, those in abject poverty lay helpless in bed as their lives draw to an end. I wanted to hug and rock them, to tell them everything would be okay, but then I noticed the nuns and volunteers who were doing exactly that. They demonstrated the patience of Job and quietly, compassionately moved through the countless beds, tending to the needs of the dying. How did they do this day after day?

We made our way to the roof and looked into streets below with all of their complexity. I could see the Kali temple and hear the sounds of an animal sacrifice. I saw dozens of beggars moving in and out of traffic and saw the dying confined to their mats on the side of the street. I was plunged back into the heartbreaking emotions I experienced before entering the Home. IF I WERE ONE OF THE NUNS, COULD I WORK HERE EVERY DAY? Where would I find the strength to continue? How COULD I FIND THAT PLACE OF PEACE INSIDE MYSELF SO I COULD SERVE THE PATIENTS?

BACK INSIDE, I CAUGHT A GLIMPSE OF HEAVEN—THERE WAS A SMALL ROOM, A CHAPEL, A SANCTUARY FILLED WITH NUNS PRAYING AND SINGING, CREATING THE MOST BEAUTIFUL ATMOSPHERE IN THE MIDST OF THE CHAOS. Peace, tranquility, order, beauty—THIS WAS THE ROOM WHERE THEY ESCAPE TO FIND THAT PEACE THAT PASSES ALL UNDERSTANDING TO CARRY WITHIN THEMSELVES TO THE DYING DESTITUTE AROUND THEM.

EDUCATING GIRLS

Girls all over the world have a tough time with their self-esteem without a loving relationship with their fathers. It is important for dads to make sure their daughters know they are valued. My heart always breaks for the middle school girl who struggles with her worth and doesn't quite know who she is. I think this uncertainty actually defines middle school girls. What would social psychologists say about the girls in India whose fathers force them to work instead of going to school, or worse, who sell them for money?

In the Indian state of Orissa, the original language does not have a word for "tomorrow." The nationals find ways to describe tomorrow, but tomorrow is not in their mental paradigm. When families struggle to eat each day, today's survival is what occupies their mind. There is no need to think about tomorrow, next month, or next year if all your time and energy is spent providing for your stomach now.

Unfortunately this mode of survival reinforces the perspective that girls should not go to school, but instead should work each day to help support the family. If there is any child from a poor family spared the daily labor of going to work, it should be a boy who could grow up and provide for the parents as they age. Why bother educating a girl if she won't be able to benefit the family as a result of her education?

I heard one father describe it this way: "If my daughter works today, she eats tonight. If she works tomorrow, she eats tomorrow night. If my daughter does not work for 50 days, then she will not eat for 50 days and die. Why bother sending her to school if she will die from it?"

This paradigm is changing now that poor girls are getting a good English education. In one village, the school had a ribbon cutting ceremony for their new permanent building after four years of existing in a temporary location. A father asked to come up on stage and requested his daughter to interpret into English what he was saying.

HE SAID THAT FOUR YEARS AGO HE ONLY THOUGHT ABOUT TODAY AND NEEDING FOOD FOR THE MEAL. HE DIDN'T UNDERSTAND THE PURPOSE OF EDUCATING A GIRL IF IT MEANT SHE COULD NOT WORK FOR THE FAMILY. He explained that if he had not sent his daughter to school, he probably would have sold her by now to help support his starving family, bUT INSTEAD HE RISKED STARVATION BY SENDING HER TO SCHOOL. NOW HE IS VERY PROUD OF HER AND UNDERSTANDS HER VALUE OUTSIDE OF PROVIDING MONEY TO THE FAMILY AND THAT SHE TOO DESERVES DIGNITY AND RESPECT.

HIS DAUGHTER WAS NOW STANDING ON A STAGE IN FRONT OF A LARGE CROWD AND SPEAKING ENGLISH. HER ABILITY TO INTERPRET HER FATHER WAS INCREDIBLE. BUT WHAT WAS SHE THINKING ABOUT HER SELF WORTH AS SHE INTERPRETED HIS WORDS?

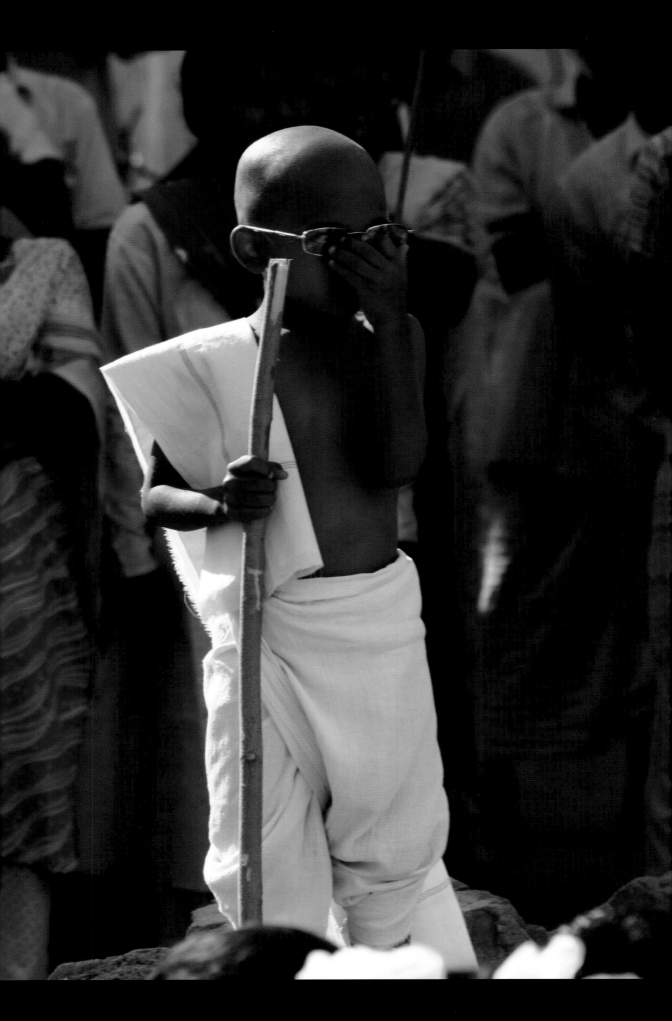

CAPTIVITY: FRIENDLY OR NOT

I had the opportunity to travel to India and work on a project for a documentary called "Friendly Captivity." The premise is that we all have things in our lives that keep us captive. We may believe we are living a free life, and in most respects we are, but inside our souls we are captives. We took seven women from Dallas and connected them to women in India who had been slaves and we recorded what happened. The women from Dallas did not know each other before the trip and they came from a variety of ethnic, religious, and economic backgrounds. The question we wanted to explore was how their lives would change if they connected to women in India.

We journeyed to the slums of Mumbai and met with women who had been rescued from the sex trafficking trade, women and children who were HIV positive, and women who had been sold or abandoned by their families. The stories that these women told were horrific and often went something like this:

A little girl lives with her family in rural India. They are extremely poor and she has several siblings. She begins working as a toddler so her family will have enough food to eat but often she does not get to eat because there is not enough food to go around. When she is ten or twelve her father or uncle tell her she is going to live in the city with a wealthy family and help them around the house. While she hates the thought of leaving her family, she is happy to think about eating every day and have a comfortable place to sleep. She is whisked away by truck and train for a day or two to a city that speaks a different language. She ends up in a lodge that has many separate bedrooms. The first night she stays there she is raped. She is raped dozens and dozens of times every night for years. Although she wants to escape, she knows she cannot go back to her home because she has been violated and is now considered "unclean." She doesn't understand the language or the systems of the city, so she doesn't have the resources to plan her escape. Prostitution now defines her life.

We had the privilege of meeting some women who had been rescued from sexual slavery and were now learning how to live outside the life of prostitution. The first moments were strained as we struggled to connect with each other. The women from Dallas were struggling with the conditions of the slums, the women from India were trying to figure out their identities as freed women, and between us, we spoke at least ten languages—where was the connecting point? With the help of interpreters, the American women began to tell their stories, explaining their lives in the United States. The ice finally broke when one lady told a joke about boyfriends and all the women in the room, Indian and American, all broke out in laughter. After that, we related more naturally, sharing stories, singing songs, giving manicures and pedicures, and connecting with each other woman to woman.

ALL OF US ARE BROKEN IN SOME WAY—VOICELESS,

ABANDONED,

POWERLESS,

SHAMED,

BUT WE ALSO HAVE THE STRENGTH AND DIGNITY TO CHOOSE TO WALK TOWARD RELATIONSHIPS AND THE INTIMACY THAT HEALS. LEARNING HOW TO MAKE A LIVING, RUN A HOUSEHOLD, OR RAISE THEIR CHILDREN WILL HELP THESE WOMEN LIVE, NOT AS SLAVES, BUT AS FREE WOMEN. But the real freedom will come when their hearts are freed from the spiritual slavery that has kept them captive, WHEN THEY CAN UNDERSTAND THAT THEY ARE WORTHY, VALUED HUMANS CREATED IN THE IMAGE OF A LOVING GOD WHO WANTS TO RESCUE THEM FROM CAPTIVITY.

ABOUT THE AUTHOR

When Nanci Ricks grew up in Indiana, she had no idea that she would be drawn to love the 250 million Dalits (Untouchables) of India. In 2001, Nanci co-founded and directed the Dalit Freedom Network (DFN), a nonprofit organization dedicated to the emancipation of India's Dalit. The Untouchables are a people group in the lowest caste, a socio-economic-religious system that relegates 25% of the Indian population to the largest form of slavery in the world. As the co-founder and former President of the Dalit Freedom Network, Nanci brings the reader along on her journeys to the villages of India. She has passionately communicated about the plight of the Dalits to countless audiences. She has testified before the US Congress as well as presented to large and small Indian and American audiences, interest groups, universities, and churches. Through her heartfelt presentations, thousands have been stirred to action for the Dalit cause in a variety of arenas. Nanci brings her experience as a Pediatric Physical Therapist, passionate visionary, published medical researcher, wound care specialist, community leader, and photographer to her artistic narrative.

In these pages, you can see her photographs and read her stories, but most importantly you will be drawn into her heart for the nation of India. While many years have passed since her first journey to the subcontinent of India, her passion for the Dalits has continued as Nanci has made more than a dozen trips to all parts of India. With a strong desire to see the world transformed, Nanci has mentored and mobilized many young leaders to look beyond their circumstances and make positive changes in the world. She is a passionate leader, developer, visionary strategist, and facilitator. As an engaging communicator, Nanci is the consummate storyteller.

To learn more and watch a slide show of her captivating photographs visit www.nanciricks.com
To reserve Nanci as a speaker at your event or display her photographic exhibit, contact nanciricks@gmail.com
To find out more about the Dalits visit www.dalitnetwork.org